UNSETTLED

KATE GRENVILLE

UNSETTLED

A journey through time and place

Black Inc.

Published by Black Inc.,
an imprint of Schwartz Books Pty Ltd
Wurundjeri Country
22–24 Northumberland Street
Collingwood VIC 3066, Australia
enquiries@blackincbooks.com
www.blackincbooks.com

9781760645649 (paperback)
9781743824009 (ebook)

A catalogue record for this book is available from the National Library of Australia

Cover design and artwork by Alex Ross
Text design, typesetting and map details by Marilyn de Castro
Main map by Alan Laver
Author photograph by Darren James

Printed in Australia by McPherson's Printing Group.

MIX
Paper from responsible sources
FSC® C001695

CONTENTS

Where this journey started *vii*

Family tree *ix*

Map *xi*

The Whale in the Rock 1

Wisemans Ferry 9

Settlers Road 31

St Albans 34

St Albans Common 38

Mogo Creek 43

Bucketty 52

Wollombi 59

Jerry's Plains 67

Murrurundi 83

Currabubula 89

Piallaway 101

The Myall Waterholes 125

Goonoo Goonoo 133

Forest Farm 146

Gunnedah 163

Gin's Leap 174

Tamworth 180

Uralla 211

Guyra 217

Myall Creek 237

Acknowledgements 247

A note about the title 251

WHERE THIS JOURNEY STARTED

I've been circling this book for years, but the subject seemed too difficult. It's about the questions that come from being a non-Indigenous person in Australia. What do we do with the fact that we're the beneficiaries of a violent past? If we acknowledge that we're on land that was taken from other people, what do we do about that?

One of the things that makes the subject difficult is the stalemate those questions end up in. Yes, the land was stolen, but the stealing happened generations ago. Should we feel guilty, or was it all too far in the past? We can't undo history, but we can't ignore it either.

Another reason not to take on those questions is that it puts us non-Indigenous Australians at the centre, where we've always been. That doesn't feel right. We might wring our hands and wonder what to do, but how can that matter in comparison with two centuries of suffering by First Nations people?

But the failure of the Voice to Parliament referendum made me decide to burrow into those hard questions in spite of the reasons not to, because the referendum was a chance to acknowledge the truth about the past and take a step towards justice, and it failed because of us non-Indigenous Australians. Sixty per cent of us voted no.

We find those questions about our place here hard to look at, let alone try to answer. *If you don't know, vote no.* That was a well-judged slogan, giving us permission to keep looking away. We can't change the past, but somehow we have to deal with what the past has bequeathed us. Sooner or later, truth needs to be told and listened to, a treaty or other agreement needs to be negotiated, and the voices of First Nations need to be heard in the places where decisions are made.

But those are big difficult things to work through. They're not something I know how to be part of. In any case I feel that, alongside the government-level movements of justice and law, something smaller needs to happen as well, something more personal. Working through those tangled issues will take an open mind, and an open mind requires an open heart.

All non-Indigenous Australians, no matter when or how they came here, benefit from the fact that this place was taken from the First Nations. Others, with different backgrounds from mine, would travel on a different path through those unsettling questions about how to be here, but thinking about my own family's footprint in this country over two centuries felt like a place where I could start. What I've done is small-scale and personal. It's open-ended and improvised. It's a journey with many detours and a few dead ends. There are no answers – just one person's attempt to look with new eyes.

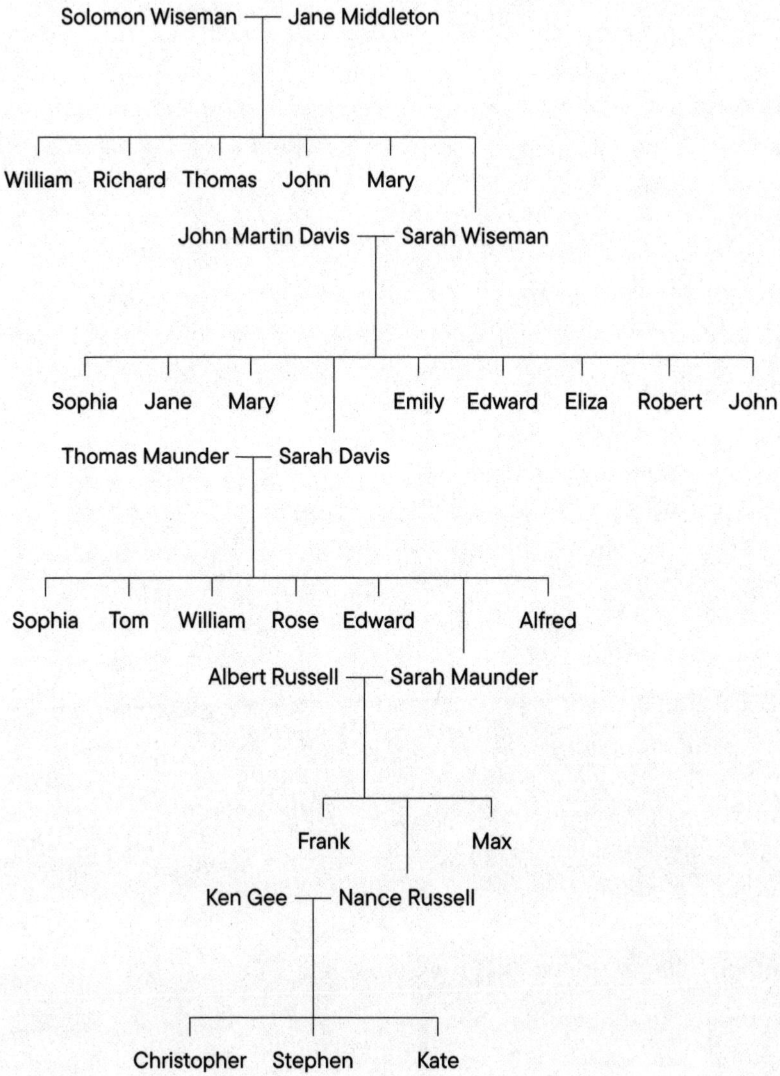
Solomon Wiseman
Jane Middleton
William
Richard
Thomas
John
Mary
John Martin Davis
Sarah Wiseman
Sophia
Jane
Mary
Emily
Edward
Eliza
Robert
John
Thomas Maunder
Sarah Davis
Sophia
Tom
William
Rose
Edward
Alfred
Albert Russell
Sarah Maunder
Frank
Max
Ken Gee
Nance Russell
Christopher
Stephen
Kate

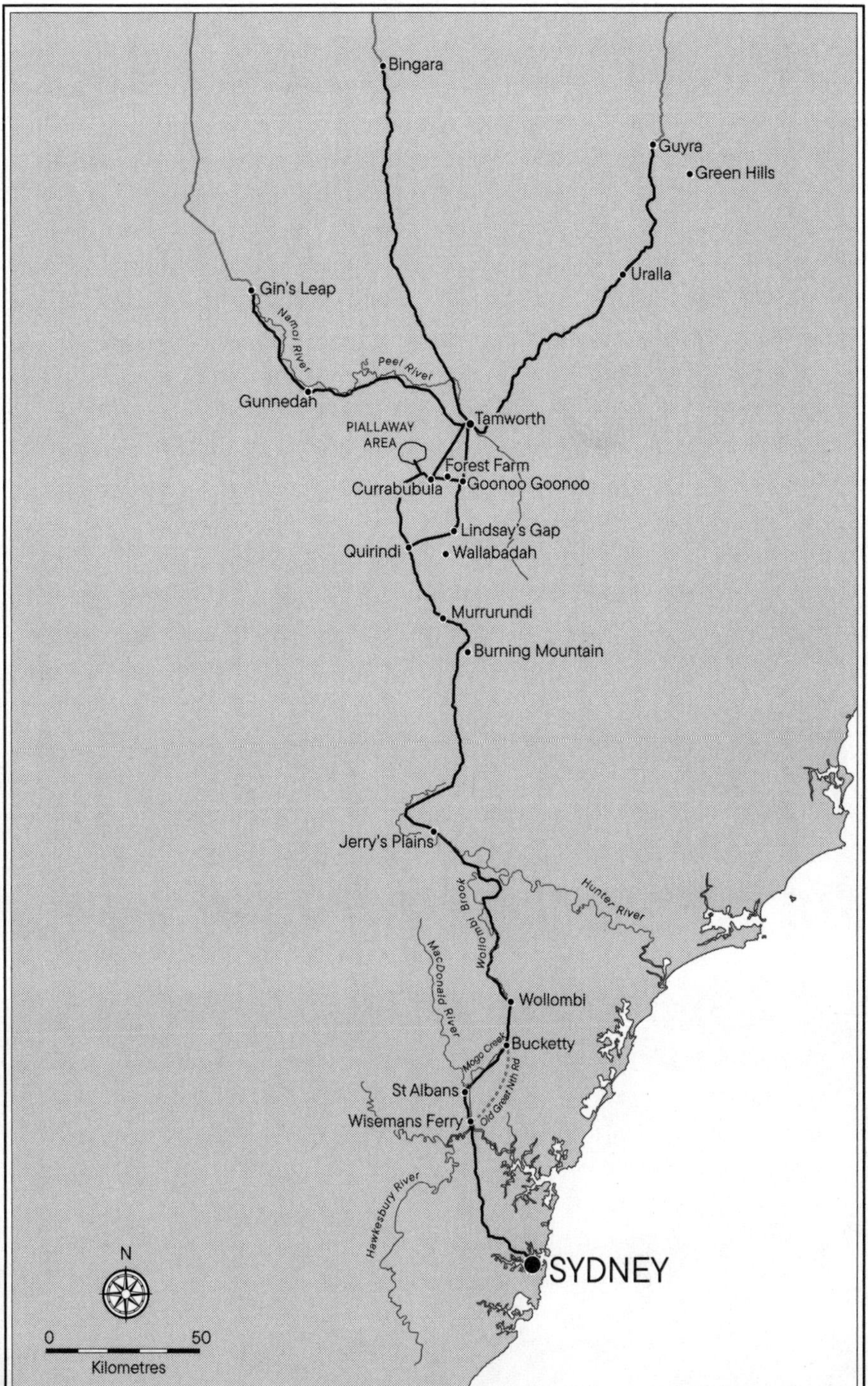

Bingara
Guyra
Green Hills
Uralla
Gin's Leap
Namoi River
Peel River
Gunnedah
Tamworth
PIALLAWAY AREA
Forest Farm
Currabubula
Goonoo Goonoo
Lindsay's Gap
Quirindi
Wallabadah
Murrurundi
Burning Mountain
Jerry's Plains
Hunter River
Wollombi Brook
MacDonald River
Wollombi
Bucketty
Mogo Creek
Old Great Nth Rd
St Albans
Wisemans Ferry
Hawkesbury River
SYDNEY
N
0
50
Kilometres

THE WHALE IN THE ROCK

I was ten or eleven when, one day in 1960 or 1961, my class walked down from North Sydney Demonstration School to Balls Head. I remember us grizzling about having to walk so far. It was hot, the sun blasting down as we trailed along.

But when we got there, we saw something that's been burned into my memory ever since, a memory as clear and undeniable as a photo. We're standing on the high point at the end of Balls Head, the harbour glittering bluely. We've left the boring suburban streets behind – out here it's all sky and sun and trees bending in the breeze. The heat beats back from a great open expanse of flat bare sandstone in front of us. Beyond it there's bush that slopes down to the harbour. There's an opening in the bushes. You can see where a track must go down the hill to the water.

We're lined up listening to the teacher because we're going to have to answer the questions on our Excursion Sheet and we're going to have to draw the thing we've come to see. Which is on the ground, behind a bright white-painted council fence. The same bright white paint has picked out a big shape engraved on the rock. It's too big to see all in one go, and unless you could levitate there's no way to get far enough away to take it all in. You have to walk around it and try to remember the shape as it disappears behind you and appears in front of you. You have to work at it.

It's nothing more than a simple outline, a whale or maybe a fish, with a tail at one end and a pointed head at the other, and fins. We're not that impressed, except by how big it is. And the fact that the council's put the fence around it.

It had been done, Mrs Linney was saying, by Aboriginal people. They'd fished in the harbour, and they'd made this whale on the rock. Not the white paint – Mrs Linney made that clear. They'd just done a groove in the rock, to make the picture. We'd put the paint there so you could see it better. And we'd put the fence around it because it was special.

I'd like to be able to say that looking at that whale on the rock was the first moment that Aboriginal people became real to me. I'd like to say it was the start of a lifetime's uncomfortable knowledge. I could pretend I felt sad, or puzzled, or curious, or sorry. But the truth is, I don't remember what I felt. Only that, of the millions of things I saw when I was ten or eleven, that's one of very few I remember. I could reconstruct that place, the bald expanse of rock, the fence, the whale-shape in stark white gloss. It seems as if I could reconstruct it molecule by molecule. So I must have felt something, but I'd be lying if said I knew what. Still, that piercingly vivid visual memory lodged in me like a splinter.

The excursion was part of a Social Studies segment about "the

Aborigines". In class we'd made paper boomerangs and drawn pictures of bark shelters. We'd made cardboard pyramids too, and drawn pictures of the Parthenon. Aboriginal people took their place alongside all those others. They were exotic and picturesque, but they were long ago. And they were gone.

That was what the engraving was telling us: *They were here, but now they're gone.* The paint and the fence were part of the message. The whale had to be painted because otherwise it would disappear. It had to be fenced to make sure we'd all know it was part of yesterday, to make sure no one mistook it for part of now.

When I was a child, the *gone* part wasn't talked about much. Measles was mentioned a lot, and so was the flu. Mostly, though, there was a sense of something inevitable, something taking its natural course, like the turning of the seasons.

These days we know a lot more about how that *going* happened. Measles and the flu played their part, but above all it was men who wanted someone else's land, and had the weapons and the hardness of spirit to use them. For the First Nations, *going* took the form of being hounded, harassed, starved, separated from kin, forced over cliffs, drowned, poisoned and shot. It meant fighting a war for their homeland over a century and a half, and resisting their dispossession right up to the present.

Until recently, the terrible story of that long war was smothered into silence, but now it's being told. These days the facts about what happened are well researched, well known and beyond dispute. For us non-Indigenous Australians, the question now isn't, *What happened?* It's, *What do we do, now that we know?*

For me it's personal. My family in this country goes back five generations, and for the first four of those generations, my forebears were on the sharp edge of the moving blade that was colonisation. With each generation, the frontier moved out from the Ground Zero of Sydney, and every time it slid further out, my family was there.

For each of those generations, there's a snippet of family story that has travelled down from mother to daughter. Each story is a sealed capsule, always told in the same words, travelling unchanged and untouched through time. The remarkable thing about those stories is how they leave out the blade. There's only one story that mentions Aboriginal people. Yet of course they were there, at every place and every time, on the country that my ancestors were taking from them.

Were my forebears part of the violence? The family stories don't tell me, though there are hints, and nor does the research I've done. But I'm prepared to assume that they were no better than any of the others.

A while ago I thought I'd go and look at that engraving again. Not with anything particular in mind, but just because the last time I'd seen it I'd known nothing about the history – the real history – of my country. I wanted to visit it again, now that I knew something of what had happened to the people who'd made that figure in the rock.

It wasn't at all what I remembered. For a start, it isn't just a whale. Inside the whale is an enigmatic human figure, legs apart, arms raised. It hadn't been picked out in white paint all those years ago and I suppose that's why it didn't become part of the picture in my memory. But looking at it now, I see that the human figure is an essential part of this work, whale-and-human joined together in some powerful and meaningful way. The council worker with the paintbrush and I had both been happy to strip away all the potent mystery from this expression of mind and spirit. We'd reduced it to an empty outline.

The other shock was that the engraving sits – and would have sat, when I first saw it – hard up against an old industrial building of uncompromising ugliness. The engraving is dwarfed by it. The windowless brick wall dominates the site.

Someone's got rid of the paint out of the engraving, but the groove that makes up the picture has a darkened, damaged look. The fence has gone too. Now there's a boardwalk above the rock. You don't have to walk around the whale trying to work it out. You can see the whole thing in a casual glance.

That memory had been so real, so undeniable, so factual for all those years, that as I stood looking down at the rock I was finding it hard to believe the evidence of my eyes. There was a dizzying gap between what I remembered and what I was looking at, and I couldn't bridge that gap. Somewhere between seeing the engraving and laying it down as a memory, I'd changed one of the most important things about it: the landscape it sat in. I'd slid the dominating industrial building away out of sight and wheeled in sky and bush and space.

Now I'd brought my neat memory-picture back here, and the place had taken it and ripped it up. It was showing me that what I'd carefully carried in my mind for so long hadn't been a memory of the actual place. It was an artefact, something I'd created for myself. I'd cleaned up the truth, erased the damage that my lot had done and the ugliness it had brought, and trivialised the engraving by leaving out half of it. The picture I'd made had allowed me to leap from what had once been here – the world this engraving was part of – straight to me standing on the same spot in the present. It allowed me to ignore what had happened in between, when, over the course of two hundred years, the world represented by the huge brick building had intruded into the world represented by the engraving.

I'd carried that artefact with me all these years and put it in place of the reality. But actual people had knelt here. Actual hands had been impelled by actual thoughts, imaginations and beliefs, and worked away at the rock. What they'd produced was an assertion of their belonging here: the physical reality of that groove carved into the rock, and the spiritual or philosophical reality of the meanings the groove carried.

Standing beside the thing that I'd misremembered so badly made an abstraction suddenly very real. It wasn't just a slogan on a t-shirt. In that moment I could feel the power of its truth through the soles of my feet. I really was on *stolen land*.

I went home with a floaty, disoriented feeling that stayed with me all evening. I made dinner and watched the news and read a book, but my mind wasn't on any of it. Something was tugging at me, some unfinished thought. If I was on stolen land, what should I do about it?

Later that night I woke up to the sound of rain rustling on the roof and chickering along the gutters, a comfortable, timeless sound of nature going about its business. I found myself thinking about this same rain falling on the engraving a few kilometres away, its naked face turned up to that gentle caress, the smooth grooves of the engraving streaming with water as the creature and its accompanying human must have in life – persisting under winter and summer, sunlight and shadow, stars and rain, that work of long-ago hands.

As sleep came to me, I realised I'd arrived at a thought. Not an answer to *What do I do?* That was too big and bossy a question. Something more modest: *Where can I start?*

I could start with where I was: myself and those family stories. I had the image of a tight little frame, and my family stories neatly enclosed within it, telling their narrow bit of truth, and then the frame expanding out and out and out. As the frame expanded it would take in the people who were here when my forebears came into their land. Not to tell their story. Not to ask them to tell it. And not to catalogue the horrors. Just to travel to the places where the family stories happened, and put the stories and those First People back into the same frame, on the same country, and see what unfolded.

The word that came to me was *pilgrimage.* I was thinking a pilgrimage is what a person might do when there was a shadow in their life that they couldn't quite look at. Setting out on a pilgrimage is a way of putting yourself in a certain frame of mind, one that makes space for open-minded musing. The body moves through space, and with it the spirit might move through understanding.

I wasn't asking myself what I hoped for or what I thought might happen. There was nothing as formed as an intention and I didn't want to try to explain it to anyone. I was going to trust whatever it was that had made me revisit that engraving. Walk on the place, that's all. And see what comes.

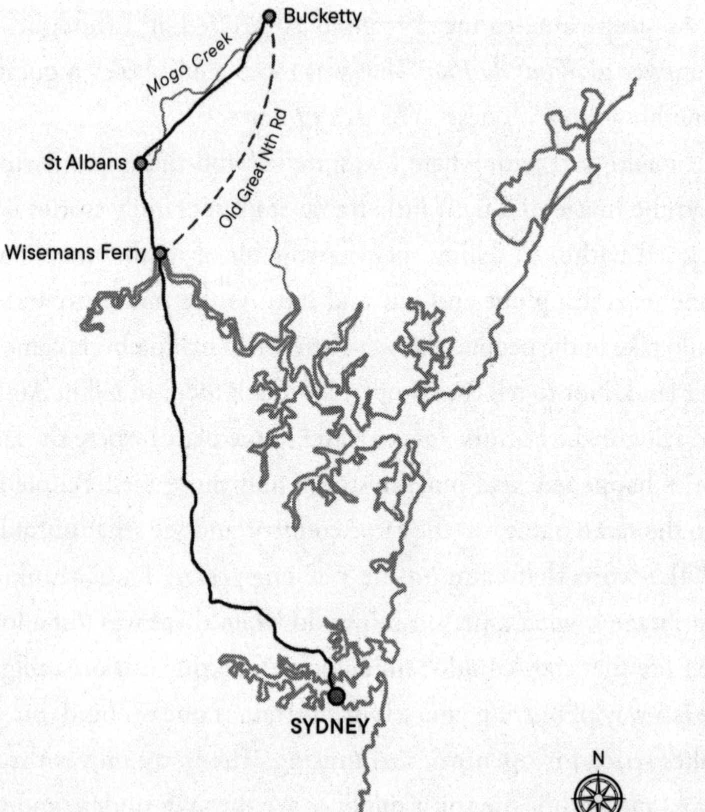
Bucketty
Mogo Creek
Old Great Nth Rd
St Albans
Wisemans Ferry
SYDNEY
N
0
20
Kilometres

WISEMANS FERRY

When my mother told the family stories, she always started with my great-great-great-grandfather Solomon Wiseman.

Solomon Wiseman was born in London and worked on the docks – he married, and for some offence we don't know of he was transported to Sydney in 1806 on the *Alexander*. His wife and young son came with him. He was freed and then took up land at what is now called Wisemans Ferry. He started the ferry, made money, built the hotel that is still there – the two lions at the gate were brought especially for the house from England.

He had a number of assigned servants, as convicts given to landowners were called. It is said he had a big rock on his property which was called "Judgement Rock" and he used

> to sit there in judgement of offenders. Even in a harsh and cruel age perhaps he was cruel – the fact remains he was hated and feared. Not that that prevented a rather flowery obituary notice from being published.
>
> His first wife died and there have always been strong rumours that he killed her by throwing her down the stairs. When we stayed there one night on the way to Sydney from Tamworth, we were shown the "haunted" room and the stairs where she was supposed to have been killed.

I've been to Wisemans Ferry many times. The first time was with Mum when I was about ten. She wanted me to see the place where the family story started, wanted me to care about it the way she did. The business about the stairs was exciting, but once the frisson of having a maybe-murderer for a relative passed, I wasn't interested.

Later, though, I was drawn back again and again to the place, circling some thoughts that were slowly taking shape as a novel, *The Secret River*, in which the central character was a fictional version of Solomon Wiseman. It had been a long journey from the ten-year-old looking at a rock engraving to a person nearly fifty years later trying to understand her country's past and share what she found with readers.

My long (and still-unfinished) education about that past began in my twenties, when I worked as editor on a documentary film about a group of Aboriginal women in South Australia – *Sister, If You Only Knew*. I met the women and heard for the first time about the reality behind the bland clichés I'd learned at school. The title of the film was as if directed straight at me: *If only you knew.* My family had been here from the earliest days of the colony, and I found that yes, I *did* want to know. Looking back at the novels I've written about the past, I can see that they're really about what I'm doing now: using the family stories as a way of trying to get beyond them to a bigger truth.

So the road to Wisemans Ferry is familiar, but I've never felt the way I do this time: that the hour's drive from Sydney is a journey backwards into deep time. You start in the densely packed houses of the city. They gradually thin out into the leafy spread-out suburbs in the north, and they thin out in turn into lifestyle blocks with horses, and bit by bit they thin out into market gardens and nurseries. All the while the road is rising. Finally, there are no more houses, no more farms, just a high plateau of dry bush. That's been there, growing and dying, growing and dying, over and over, for endless stretches of the past.

On one of those earlier visits – more than twenty years ago now – I was told that this road was originally an Aboriginal track. I didn't pay much attention then, but today I'm very conscious of it. The road looks as if it slices through this thin bush at its own convenience, laying down its bitumen, painting its white line down the middle, carving imperiously through rock and dirt. But under all that pushy stuff is the timeless logic of the landscape. On either side of the road the land falls away steeply. If you'd wanted to travel north any time in, say, the last sixty thousand years, you'd have followed this level ridge. Sitting in my bubble of comfort and speed, I'm making exactly the journey across the land that people have been making since there were people here to make it. For all its assertive footprint, this road doesn't lead. It follows.

Just before you get to Wisemans Ferry, there's a lookout perched high on the edge of the escarpment. I stop, as I've stopped every time I've come here, and walk to the edge. I look out with – what is it? – I want to say *fear*. This isn't a cosy or friendly landscape. Below me, the land falls away in a steep slope where huge shelves and outcrops of rock burst through the stony soil and the trees are thin, barely holding on. Way, way down is the river, wide and glittering with a hard metallic light. The First People here, the Dharug and the Darkinjung, called it Dyarubbin. The colonists called it after one of their masters, Lord Hawkesbury.

And there are the cliffs. Over the aeons the river has sliced its way down through a tremendous thickness of sandstone so that on the far side, the stream now runs at the base of towering, ragged walls of rock that plunge straight into the water. You can see how the stone was laid down, horizontal layer by horizontal layer of sand being deposited and compressed over unimaginable stretches of time. Weather has worked away at that piling up of layers so that now the whole mighty face of the cliff is a mass of overhangs and undercuts, pieces fallen away to show ruptures of fresh gold in among the bulges and buckles of weathered grey. Written all over it like some delicate fluid script are the bending, twisting, pale trunks of spindly trees.

There's something hypnotic about those mighty cliffs. I keep searching for a sense of scale – how big are those trees? What would a human look like against that wall of rock? The eye is desperate to find a pattern among the baffling jumble of gold and grey. The calligraphy of the trees leads the gaze now here, now there, straining to find meaning in the small crisp lines drawn against the jumble of the rock.

Time has written its history here. It's magnificent and majestic and dramatic, but it's daunting. It's a landscape that's not on a human scale. Here the vast engine of weather has worked with the vast engine of time to tell a simple story: *Be humble, humans.*

The village of Wisemans Ferry sits at the bottom of the escarpment, within an enormous loop in the river curving around a spread of flat land. There's not much there: a post office, a pub, a scattering of houses and a few shops. It's very quiet. The air is humid and somehow thick. The light has a glary grey quality.

He started the ferry, made money, built the hotel that is still there. The hotel dominates the village, a strongly built cube of stone, two storeys with verandahs top and bottom – the gracious architecture that, in early colonial Australia, was the way to tell everyone you'd done well. Wiseman commissioned a picture of it, *Mr Wiseman's Villa.* The picture includes all the trappings of his wealth: the horses, the cattle, the formal garden with the fountain and a high white wall all around, and at the centre of it, the man sitting on the verandah at his ease, a servant bending over him.

Solomon Wiseman was born in Bermondsey, at that time a grim working-class part of London. He was a lighterman on the Thames and one night in 1805 he was caught stealing some valuable timber. A year later he was transported for the term of his natural life to New South Wales. On arrival he was assigned to his wife as a convict servant and soon earned his ticket-of-leave and then a pardon. Over the next thirty years he made a lot of money from various businesses, finishing here with a ferry across the river, an inn, and a finger in many other lucrative pies.

He was freed and then took up land at what is now called Wisemans Ferry. This is where he did that. This, right here, is the actual, specific bit of land that he *took up*. And what a weasel word of a phrase that is. What Wiseman actually did was that he *took* the land.

How interesting, that we've added that little word *up* to *took*. It makes all the difference in the world. *Took* is blunt. The picture is of a grab. But *took up* – you *take up* a suggestion or a bit of unfinished knitting. *Took up* suggests something that's been neglected or abandoned. You're going to finish the job and look after it properly.

That first day, Wiseman probably knew that the people he'd have called *blacks* or *black natives* already lived on the land he wanted to take, because they'd have been there, or somewhere in the area, with their fires and huts, when he landed. They lived there for the same reasons he wanted to – in the dry stoniness all around, it was an oasis where humans could flourish. Wallabies and roos and emus came down to the river to drink and graze and could be speared. Possums that lived in the big old trees by the water could be smoked out. The gently shelving banks gave a footing for people fishing and somewhere to launch a bark canoe.

And the fertile soil by the river was perfect for growing a small unassuming plant with a root that's good to eat. The First People of this area called them midyini, though they're more often known by the name they go by further south: murnong. They were a staple of Aboriginal people's diet in many parts of the country – they'd be dug up and eaten, but a part of the root would be planted for the next crop. When I was researching for *The Secret River*, a Dharug man described them to me and explained about the replanting. *Just exactly like an Irishman with a potato*, he said, and let that thought sink in.

The people who lived there – like those who lived everywhere else in what's now called Australia – had a relationship to their land for which there's no equivalent in non-Indigenous culture. It's often expressed as "the people belonging to the land, rather than the land belonging to the people". My understanding of it is that the landscape was, and is, the embodiment of a vast and timeless spiritual reality. The identity and meaning of any individual human life is profoundly connected to a particular tract of country and the stories about its features. It's more than living on it, more than knowing it, more than being sustained by it, more than loving it, though it's all of those. It's an inextricable, inseparable, existentially vital part of who a person is and where they fit in the cosmos.

But Wiseman knew nothing of that kind of relationship to a place. He wanted that curve of land on the river, and what he had in mind was what was familiar to him: ownership. In London he'd been at the bottom of the heap, living hungrily from hand to mouth. He'd never have dreamed of being the possessor and master of a piece of the earth. But here it was possible, even expected, for a man to *take up* land. Take it, and work out later what to do about the fact that it was already the home – and spiritual identity – of other people.

It's a strange feeling to walk up the stone steps to the verandah and sit exactly where my great-great-great-grandfather sits in the picture. An ugly strip of shops has been built across the bottom of his garden and these days they're all you can see when you look out, but when Wiseman sat here he'd have been able to gaze down the slope all the way to the river and the cliffs, as ever-changing under the light coming and going as an expressive face. And down there, past the fountain and the rose garden, he'd have been able to admire his corn growing strongly in the deep fertile soil beside the river.

When he first came here, that good soil would have been where the midyini plants grew. He'd have dug them up and thrown them aside so he could plant his corn. Like most of the foreigners here, he was doing his best to replicate how things were back home in England. He might or might not have known what the Dharug called their crop. But he'd definitely have known that the plants were food, because he'd have called them by the name all the colonists used: *yam daisies*. That name tells you something his great-great-great-granddaughter would be more comfortable not knowing: Wiseman would have understood that those plants were eaten by the people who lived here. But he dug them up anyway.

Sitting up here in the middle of the picture of *Mr Wiseman's Villa* could be a cosy nostalgic feeling, a pleasurable continuity and connection. But it's not. That's because I've learned a bit about what happened on the Hawkesbury during the years that Wiseman was sitting here.

Along this fertile stretch of the river Aboriginal people had gathered for many centuries, perhaps at times different groups together, observing the proper protocols and courtesies required by the act of sharing the land. But when Wiseman and the other foreigners arrived, they were ignorant of any of that, and they weren't thinking about sharing, only of owning. The place acquired boundaries where it had never had boundaries before, fences and walls and other invisible borders that Aboriginal people crossed at their peril. The midyini was dug up, the game was frightened away, the big possum-trees were cut down, and in their place were the corn and the pigs and the sheep brought by the foreigners.

At the time Wiseman arrived, the river was the frontier, the place where the foreigners were pushing in and Aboriginal people were pushing back. There's an ample historical record to show there was violence on both sides. Aboriginal people were fighting for their homeland, and the British were fighting for land they wanted. Governor Macquarie set up heavily armed garrison towns along the river to protect the settlers. When that didn't do the trick, he published a declaration that essentially gave permission to settlers to shoot any Aboriginal people who came near their farms.

But did it happen right here, where I'm sitting? Was my great-great-great-grandfather one of the foreigners who felt entitled to get out his gun to defend what he called his? Would he have understood, when the roos were frightened away and a sheep was speared instead, or when corn was taken from the place where the midyini had grown? Or would he have puffed himself up with righteous English indignation, and punished as thieves and trespassers the people who'd eaten it?

Wiseman was illiterate, but he employed a clerk to fire off letters – to the government asking for things, mostly, or to other white men on the river, asserting his rights. I've read those letters, and the many other documents from the time that mention him. In those hundreds of pieces of paper, there's not a single reference to Aboriginal people, much less how Wiseman dealt with them.

If you wanted to reassure yourself, you'd say that's good. That means nothing bad happened on Wiseman's particular length of the frontier. Or you could say the silence tells you the worst. If you'd been part of the violence, would you record what you did? Would you sit by the fireside with your children in your lap and tell them about it, so they could pass it on to their children?

I've thought about what I'd feel if I knew for certain that he picked up the gun, and what I'd feel if I knew for certain that he didn't, and I've realised that, in the big picture, it doesn't make all that much difference. Whatever my particular, individual forebear did or didn't do, he was part of the relentless flood of foreigners who eventually pushed into every corner of the continent. Over many years they did their best to push out the people who were there. Took their country, their livelihood, their children and often their lives. I've accepted that that puts me on the side of a great wrong. I didn't do it, and it's possible that my great-great-great-grandfather didn't commit any of the violence. All the same, I'm part of it, because I've benefitted from it.

I'm glad my family isn't still here, that after Wiseman died there were no more Wisemans at Wisemans Ferry. I'm only now realising how uncomfortable I've always felt in this village, even when I was coming here so often in search of starting points for the novels. Partly it's the slightly suffocating quality of the air and the way the valley presses in so narrowly, cliffs on one side rearing above you and plunging straight down into the water, the great rocky mass of ridge on the other. I can admire the grandeur. I can see it's beautiful. But wherever you look, the eye is stopped. The word *claustrophobic* comes to mind.

Every time I've been here I've been restless to leave. Today I'm queasy, uneasy, full of a generalised dread. I realise it's not because of the cliffs or the humid air. It's not about the place. It's about what I know. For me, this is a haunted landscape, haunted by a past that's all the darker for the things that were never recorded.

Since I was here last, someone has considered Solomon Wiseman worthy of a bronze statue. It's outside the pub, near the lions on the gateposts. Perhaps it's because most bronze statues are a bit larger than life-sized, but the bronze Wiseman seems a bit runty.

Personally, as his descendant, I feel nothing but distaste for the statue and all it stands for. He left his stamp on this bend of the river, but that doesn't make him someone to be honoured. He was no hero and by all accounts not a good man. The family story keeps it vague as to whether the wife-killing was an accident, and when I was researching I discovered that the stairs she was supposed to have fallen down weren't built when she died. That made me wonder whether there was any truth at all in the story, but you hear a variant of it from the locals. They say she fell over the upstairs balcony railing onto the stone steps below, and the suggestion is that it wasn't an accident.

There's a plaque, mercifully terse: *Solomon Wiseman, Pioneer innkeeper, ferrymaster*. There's a lot of stuff on another plaque about the convict-built Great North Road that ran through the township. Not a word – not a single solitary word! – about the Dharug or the Darkinjung.

That word *pioneer* makes me remember a newspaper story I came across in my research, a story that had taken place at around Wiseman's time here, in a riverside village not far away. It was so vivid and odd that I'd tried to adapt it for the novel. In the end I didn't use it, but the scene stuck in my mind.

A well-hit ball went into long grass and was swallowed by a snake. The batsman killed the snake with his bat, retrieved the ball and play was resumed.

So it's Sunday afternoon and the blokes aren't dressed in white or anything but they're playing the quintessentially English game. It's hot and humid and they've only cleared a small patch in the long grass, so people aren't trying to hit a six, but they're going to play the game that says, *The English are here*. We are not going to be awed by those mighty cliffs, or the seething river, or the flies and mosquitos and snakes and leeches. Not to mention the birds that laugh at us. We've brought ourselves here, and we've brought the entire baggage of our culture with us, every antimacassar and piano and cricket set, and by Jove, we're going to let this place know who's boss.

Someone hits the ball a bit harder than he meant to and it sails out past the cleared patch, into the long grass. There's laughing, bantering, the men all go into the grass looking for the ball. It's a precious item, expensive, and not in ready supply here, a long voyage by boat from where cricket balls are made. After a while everyone runs out of jokes and the laughing stops. There's no sign of the ball. The place has – as usual! – ruined an Englishman's fun.

Then one of the blokes walks away, faces up to a tree and has a piss against it, and it's while he's buttoning himself up that he sees it – a bent length of something on the ground, gleaming darkly like polished wood. A snake. And a little way from the head, a bulge the exact size and shape of a cricket ball.

The bugger's eaten the ball, he shouts. The others don't believe him, they have to come and see for themselves. The snake's trying to get away but the men make a ring of stamping boots around it. You can see the cricket ball is slowing it down, but any minute it will get away. Go on, mate, someone shouts to the man still holding the bat. Get the bugger, quick!

Everyone watches him jab. Once, and the snake writhes, twists, turns over so they can see the dull yellow of its belly. Twice, and the head's lying mashed in the dust. A cheer goes up. Play is resumed.

The ball was swallowed by a snake. Really? In a snake zoo I once watched a snake eat a dead mouse. It took quite a while and I wouldn't use the word *swallow* to describe what happened. From where I was standing, it looked as if the mouse stayed still and the snake gradually pulled itself over it. The snake didn't swallow the mouse as much as engulf it.

And would a snake be that stupid, anyway, to eat a cricket ball?

The batsman killed the snake with his bat. Now I don't want to boast, but I've actually killed a snake, and I wouldn't want to have done it with a cricket bat. Even a snake with a cricket ball in its innards could move fast. You'd want to keep as much distance as you could between you and it. A cricket bat isn't long enough for comfort, and it's a clumsy sort of shape for hitting something lying flat along the ground. You'd have to jab with the end of the bat, and it would be hard to get enough force behind the jab.

But okay, these are tough blokes. They'd have killed more snakes than I have.

What about that casual *retrieved the ball*? If the ball had got any distance down the snake, which is what *swallowed* means, it wouldn't be a matter of reaching in and tweaking the ball out. You'd have to cut it out. Well, those are the sort of blokes who'd always have a knife with them, I suppose. A pouch on their belt. So one of them whips out his knife. A snake's skin is tough. It might have taken two of them, one bloke to hold the body and the other to saw away. By the time that ball was *retrieved* everything would be pretty messy.

But *play was resumed.* What a splendid tone of manly insouciance that's got!

Call me a spoilsport, but now, thinking about the actuality of the moment rather than the words in the newspaper, I've parted company with the whole thing. Some journalist needed to fill a few column inches with something light. *Play was resumed* – you can hear the tongue-in-cheek tone that says, *Get the joke?*

It's a joke, but it's a bit of propaganda too, though that would have been so deeply in the journalist's bones he wouldn't have known he was carrying it. It's another ripping yarn about *our brave pioneers.* About calm British competence triumphing over a weird hostile place. About not letting the place beat you, no matter what it threw at you. About a place you couldn't quite take seriously, a place with snakes silly enough to eat a cricket ball. All part of the new-hatched national myth about the easy superiority of the newcomers and, between the lines, how that gave them the right to be there.

To get away from the pressed-in village and the bronze statue that I wish wasn't here, I walk down the hill towards the river, past the shops, past the bowls club, past the war memorial. *Valour* on one side of the weather-worn soldier in his slouch hat, *Honour* on the other, *Lest We Forget* across the middle.

On my earlier visits to Wisemans Ferry there'd been a playing field here, and a park-like area of open bush and long grass where you could walk right down to the edge of the river. I'd stood there one hot morning, marvelling at the muscular current flowing between its banks, the cliffs towering over me, and thought about the fact that on the day he landed and decided to claim this place, Solomon Wiseman would have stood more or less exactly where I was standing, and seen more or less exactly what I was seeing. He'd have seen his future here – better than his past! – using this river that was much the same size and tidal temperament as the one he knew back home. People had needed to cross the Thames, and they'd need to cross this one too. He'd be the man to ferry them across.

I'd spent time in the pub talking to the publican, I'd heard all the stories about the ghost of the first Mrs Wiseman. I'd even spent a restless – though ghost-free – night in the room where she was supposed to appear. But what I needed before I could write the book was something with more substance than a ghost story. I needed to make Wiseman's story a concrete part of the present – for that long-ago past to feel real enough for me to believe it.

I'd read that his first ferry was downstream from the current one and I'd spent a lot of time one morning crouched in the grass by the river, the wannabe archaeologist in me in full cry, looking for evidence of that long-vanished punt. I remember how hot and humid it was and the feel of the sun on my back as I crouched here, scraping away with a piece of twig, intent on my tiny world of old dirt, determined to find a bit of the past that I could hold in my hand.

At home I've got a box called *Objets Mostly Wiseman*, full of the things I picked out of the dirt that day. They're nothing much. A piece of wood tunnelled with holes, that I convinced myself was a fragment of the first ferry, eaten by the worms that were the bane of old wooden boats. An enormous rusty square nail – yes, exactly the kind of thing that could have held the old ferry together! A bit of something vaguely round, vaguely flat – oh, a long-lost button! The little grey thing that I imagined as a button is probably just an odd-shaped pebble, but it's in the box with the rest of the bits, in an envelope carefully labelled with the date I scratched it out of the dirt.

But standing here now, twenty years later, I don't much care about Solomon Wiseman or his ferry. The bit of wormy wood, the nail, the maybe-button – they were the last, shallowest, least significant layer of the place. What I'm seeing today is that here – right here – is where the midyini would have grown. That dirt I scratched away at so intently – it was fine, dark, alluvial soil, the deposits of a thousand floods. That rich soil made it the best place for the midyini to be planted. Planted, and dug up to be eaten, raw or roasted, and planted and dug up again, for generation after generation.

Twenty years ago did I know about midyini? Yes, but they weren't real to me, not as real as a bit of old stuff that might have been a button. I'd glanced at a few muddy pictures of them in books but I'd never actually seen one. They were interesting and explained a lot about the conflict along the river, but they were nothing to do with me and you couldn't pick them up and put them carefully in an envelope and label it with the date, because they weren't there anymore. The foreigners had dug them up so efficiently that they're now locally extinct.

But a few years ago I happened on a native-plant nursery that sold seedlings of midyini. That shouldn't have been surprising, but it was. In fact it was a shock, as if I'd just seen Napoleon in the IGA checkout line. I bought a few and planted them in my little garden, and although they didn't thrive, they grew. There were the curved stalks I'd seen in the pictures, with the little flowers on their ends tilting as if modestly glancing down at the ground. When the plants seemed to have finished their season I dug them up. My crop was too tiny to be worth roasting, but I washed the dirt off the translucent roots and ate them. Crisp of texture, delicate of flavour. I could imagine that when roasted they'd be nutty and satisfying.

It made me realise that midyini weren't like Napoleon. My forebear had tossed them aside, and in relegating them to the status of dead museum pieces I'd done something not so very different. Standing here now, the reality of this riverside place as a midyini field is powerfully present to me. There I was, scratching away obsessively for a few bits of rubbish, when all around me were the ghosts of a thousand nodding yellow flowers dancing in the breeze.

I walk back to the village, trudging past *Lest We Forget* and on up the hill. I'm trying to understand how I'd stood on this place all those years ago and not seen what it had to show me. How had I missed it? I'm shocked at myself, confused, irritable.

As I pass the shops I notice a sign advertising locally made pottery and art. It reminds me that I need a gift for a family member. Lily will like something handmade, and anyone trying to make a living from pottery or art in this out-of-the-way place will be glad of a sale.

Up the steps and into the shop. I'm the only customer. The shop's terribly quiet. I wander around looking at mugs and jugs, tea-towels and hats and paintings of birds. The woman behind the counter lets me wander for a while but perhaps the silence is getting to her too.

Let me know if you'd like any help, won't you? she says. Any information. About anything.

Oh yes, thanks, I say. Lovely things.

Then the silence folds down on us again.

At last I find something that I think Lily might like and take it over to the counter.

Oh, this is lovely, isn't it, the woman says, and I agree. Then I notice that right in front of me, on a shelf level with my knee, are copies of some of my own books. I keep my hat on and my head down. I don't want her to glance up and say, Oh, but you're Kate Grenville! I recognise you from the books!

Now, why don't I?

The books are the ones set right here, on the very ground that my great-great-great-grandfather *took up*. They're about fictionalised versions of Solomon Wiseman and his family. They draw a picture of what might have happened here between black and white when the *taking up* thing was starting to unfold.

Standing here where those events were set, I don't want to have a smiling conversation about them. Not those books, those stories, that history. I'm proud of the books. But I'm not proud of the history.

She scuffles around, peeling off the price sticker, rustling about with a piece of orange tissue paper that I can see has been used before and it's creased, so it's resisting the new creases she's trying to make. As she folds one end in the other pops out, and the sticky tape doesn't seem to be helping.

I'm better at weaving than wrapping things up, she says with a laugh. Glances at me. She's angling for a bit of conversation, a bit of friendly nothing – it must be boring here with no customers all day.

Then I see that there are a few woven bowls on the counter. She probably made them and she'd probably like me to buy one. On another day, I would. But I've put myself in some kind of a mood, what with the bronze statue and the midyini that used to be there and aren't anymore – it's a hot muddle of confused feelings of I-don't-quite-know-what. And somehow it seems important to stay with that confusion. Somehow it feels as if that's what I'm here for. I don't want to smooth it away with a bit of affable chitchat.

She finally plasters enough tape on the thing to make the paper stick, takes my credit card. As she snaps off the paper receipt from the machine and hands it to me with a *thanking you!* I see a sharpness in her movements and hear a tightness in her voice. I've been feeling cranky and confused, and now I've infected her. She'll go home and tell her husband, You know a woman came in today, my goodness, she must have got up on the wrong side of the bed!

It's only when I've left, having so gracelessly rebuffed her conversational openings, that I realise her woven dishes are very like a bowl I once bought in the Northern Territory. It didn't occur to me as we were talking, but now I think, Is she Aboriginal? Did I miss an opportunity there? Maybe I should have got talking with her, discussed what I was doing. Maybe this is a repeat of the way I didn't think enough about the midyini all those years ago.

In that moment at the foot of the steps, hesitating about whether to turn back and talk to her, I'm trying to work out how I should do this *pilgrimage*. I could talk to people all the way along. Strike up conversations, listen to what they tell me. Take up opportunities, like the one the woman in the shop was offering me.

From when I first started to write books set in colonial times, I've asked for help and advice from Aboriginal people. I've always approached them diffidently, because I knew I was just one more in an endless line of white people wanting something from them: information, stories, a connection to their world. And I felt that they shouldn't be asked to get involved in what I regard as our problem. The toxic legacy of colonisation is something our forebears made. At least for a time, I think it's right for us to do our soul-searching on our own.

Conversations and consultations are important and respectful. But they can also be a trespass on someone else's pain. At times, too, they can feel close to asking for an unearned reassurance or even forgiveness.

The people I've spoken with over the years have been unfailingly patient and generous. There are so many things that we white people don't understand. When that Dharug man told me that what his people had done was *just like an Irishman with a potato*, it was a revelation. It was a central fact to understanding the situation I was trying to write about.

But my books aren't about Aboriginal people, they're about us non-Indigenous Australians. After all, it was our forebears who came here and did the damage. It's our attitudes, our words, our frames of reference, that keep on blocking the way forward. And yet we've looked away from that. From our position at the centre of things – the ones with the power – we've looked out at the people we displaced and seen them as something we had to do something about: the *Aboriginal issue* or the *Aboriginal problem*. We've sometimes looked outwards with good intentions. The phrase *acknowledgement of country* trips off our tongues these days, and acknowledgement is a good thing to be doing. It's taken us two hundred years to get that far. But there's a sense that it's something we're doing *for* First Nations people. At best it's a respectful courtesy, at worst it's tokenism, but whatever it is, it's a way of looking away from ourselves and what we've done.

There at the centre, we've been invisible to ourselves and unconscious of ourselves, the way no one's conscious of the air they're breathing, or the fact that they're breathing it. Making this journey might be about trying to – as you might say – become conscious of the air. About watching myself breathing it. About stepping back and looking at the past, and watching myself looking at it. About turning the gaze back to those attitudes, those words, those frames of reference, and bringing them to consciousness.

I think all that can only happen on my own. Making connections with people is essential. I've done that in the past and I'll do it again. But I don't think it's what I'm doing this time. Whatever it is that I'm doing, it feels like a private, exploratory thing. I don't want to have to try to explain it – I want to leave it unarticulated, to leave a space for something to enter. I'd learn one kind of thing by having conversations with people. But I have a feeling that I'll learn another kind of thing by going through this on my own.

Outside the shops, wrapped gift in hand, I look up and down the empty street as if I'm expecting something. It's a relief to decide that I've seen enough of Wisemans Ferry. On the far side of the river, another, smaller, river joins the Hawkesbury and bends off among the hills. The First People called it Gunanday. The colonists called it the First Branch. Now it's called the MacDonald River. There's where the next part of the family story is going to take me.

SETTLERS ROAD

As Wiseman's six children grew up, he didn't send them to school because, he said, as the children of a convict they'd be humiliated. In any case, what was the good of reading and writing? Better, he said, to give your children flocks and herds and help them find land to run them on.

So as the Wiseman boys came of age, in the second decade of the nineteenth century, they took their stock across the river on their father's punt and headed up the valley of the First Branch. They weren't planning to settle along that stream because there were limited patches of good land there, and in any case, most of it was already settled by small-scale men on hardscrabble farms. The Wiseman boys knew there were better pickings further north, broad fertile valleys that no one had *taken up*. The valley of the First Branch was the easiest way to get there.

I'm going along the same path they'd have followed, now a narrow strip of bitumen that heads north. It's called Settlers Road, and that's exactly what it was. The river loops around, and in the elbow of every bend there's another triangle of fertile land. Millennia of dirt has washed down out of the hills and been swept down the river in floods, and it's pooled in these corners and drained and left something as level as a horizon. I'm imagining the first *settlers* here feeling they couldn't believe their luck. They'd have struggled around the shoulder of a harsh dry hill and found a place ready-made for them, already a deep-soiled flat paddock that only needed to be scratched over, the yam daisies dug out, and the corn seeds trodden into the soft dirt. And another around the next shoulder – a string of beads of green along the winding stream. Now and then there's a lagoon where the river's changed course and left a bit of itself behind. And all around, at the back of every patch of that green, the walls of the stony hills rear up into the sky.

When the foreigners like Wiseman took up the best land, along the main river, and were given tacit permission to hound away the Dharug and the Darkinjung, these smaller chips of land might have been places for those people to retreat to. But not for long. Year by year, bend by green bend, hostile boundary by hostile boundary, they'd have been forced further and further up the valley. As I drive on, the road swivels high around a spur of land and opens into yet another triangle of green and I have a sudden vivid sense of Aboriginal people here. With each further corner they retreated to, I wonder if they thought, Surely the foreigners have enough now? But the foreigners never had enough. The First People fought back, but they were chivvied from one sweet nook to another until the white men filled every corner of the valley.

The chips of flat land were too small to support many settlers. In 1831, when someone counted them, there were only eighty-six colonists along the whole length of Settlers Road. This valley with its modest stream still feels like a backwater of a backwater. One of its offshoots is actually called Forgotten Valley.

Those few scattered settlers weren't people of learning. They didn't leave much in writing about what went on between themselves and the people they were displacing, but there are stories. When I was dodging around here twenty years ago, I got talking with a local man whose great-great-great-grandfather – another lighterman from the Thames – had probably known my own great-great-great-grandfather. He was telling me about the old days along Settlers Road. The farms, how hard the life was on the remote little plots. The lagoons, full of ducks, fish, and the eels that his great-great-great-grandfather had sworn would cure anything that ailed a man. I happened to mention a particular lagoon I'd noticed as I'd driven past, a beautiful stretch of sparkling water in a fold in the land, with a neat white fence and a big house on a rise. As the most casual thing in the world he said, Oh, yes, that place. That was the site of the last massacre.

He didn't mean to say it. It had slipped out, and he'd have unsaid it if he could. He covered it over straight away with a cross-hatching of half-denials. Oh, it was only a rumour. Just something people said. You know the way people are. And did you know they used to bake possum in a hollowed-out pumpkin?

Well, yes. When two sets of people want the same land, I think we do know *the way people are.*

ST ALBANS

Settlers Road ends at the hamlet of St Albans, some 20 ks north of Wisemans Ferry. The other St Albans, the one in England that this one was named after, is considerably grander than this one. There are no Roman walls here, no hoards of buried gold. This St Albans is a handful of modest houses scattered on a rise above the river. Some of them are B&Bs for weekend getaways, some of them are arty endeavours with handmade signs advertising pottery and jewellery. The woman who made the woven bowls that I didn't buy might live in one of them.

But the heart of St Albans is the pub, a big place built – as the tourist come-on boasts – of *convict-hewn sandstone* in 1836. It's called the Settlers' Arms, a name I'd never normally give a second thought to. But today, settlers like my forebears, who might or might not have been bearing *arms* and might or might not have been prepared to use them, are on my mind. Given what may well have happened in this valley, it occurs to me that the name could be a bit of an in-joke.

Oh, don't be silly. That's a modern person reading too much into an ordinary old pub tradition. All those English pubs called the Somebody-or-Other's Arms aren't talking about arms in the sense of weapons, but in the sense of coats-of-arms.

Which, now I think about it, *are* about weapons.

Now I think about it. That's the thing – I'm thinking about things now, rather than sliding along on the well-lubricated surface of unremarkable words. Thinking in a way that allows a whole other story to be glimpsed. No, not even a story, just a suggestion or a suspicion, embedded so far below the surface it's easy to pooh-pooh it as ridiculous.

The minute I step into the pub I feel uneasy. Partly it's because I'm old enough to remember when women weren't allowed to be served in the public bar of any pub in Australia. We had to make do with the Ladies' Lounge, usually a grim place smelling of mildew. We could hear the happy hubbub of the men in the front bar but we couldn't join them. It was like being outside a party you hadn't been invited to. Whatever blokes we were with would buy us a drink and sit with us for a while, but they'd soon find an excuse to slip back to where the fun was.

In my twenties – the 1970s – I was part of a group of uppity women's libbers who went into the public bar of a Sydney hotel and demanded to be served. It ended up in a barney with the publican, of course. That was the point. We wanted a barney, wanted to draw attention. Shouting – angry women never sound impressive, our voices are too shrill – while the men in the bar watched us, their faces heavy with scorn and contempt, not needing to get involved because they knew they had the law on their side.

I can vividly remember the transgressive glee of marching up to the bar, can hear us screeching at the publican, remember rapping on the counter with a coin, demanding to be served. I've even got a clear memory of the long hippy skirt I was wearing. I can visualise the brave start all right, but the funny thing is, I can't visualise the way the thing ended. The only thing I know is that the publican threatened to call the cops and all the puff went out of us.

When you're ashamed, when you wish you'd been braver and done something differently, it's amazing how memory fades.

Here in the Settlers' Arms in the present day there's no problem with a woman walking into a pub, but as soon as I go through the low doorway I feel ill at ease. Finding my way to the bar feels like being drawn through a maze of small rooms and alcoves and corridors and sudden turnings like traps. There's a feeling of something tight, small, old, shadowy, closed-in, behind those thick stone walls. In the bar a few men, rusted-on locals by the look of them, turn and have a good old stare before they go back to their glasses. There's a powerful smell of stale beer. In a corner an ancient man is blowing his nose slowly and thoroughly into a big handkerchief.

The claim to fame of the Settlers' Arms, why weekend visitors make the trek here, is that it's *heritage.* There are lots of Ye Olde things on the walls, bits of rusty machinery and dim black-and-white photos of *pioneers.* Oh, what a lot of hooey, I think. What does *heritage* really mean? It means what we've inherited, what belongs to us, what we're part of. *Heritage* means it's ours, and what's being celebrated in this old pub is its our-ness. Here in this valley, at the end of a long narrow road, hemmed in by those timeless ridges of land, I can see why we'd want to make a big song and dance about *heritage*. Big though the pub is, thick though the walls are, it's nothing more than a speck of something foreign in the immense old landscape pressing in on all sides.

I'm turning the word *hooey* over, relishing its old-fashioned scorn. *Hooey.* It's not a word I ever use and I wonder why it's come to my mind now – is it because the word itself is a bit of *heritage*?

The barman glances at me and I think, Oops, did I just say hooey out loud? He turns away, but the moment makes me listen to myself, how much I'm enjoying my scorn. What right do I have to be scornful? My being scornful is just one more way of denying that I'm part of all that hooey about *pioneers.* I don't use that word for them, but my forebears were just like the men up in the photos on the walls. And although I've set off on this trip with the idea of going somewhere new, couldn't it also be said that I'm just following all those other descendants of pioneers who obsessively burrow into their family history as part of their *heritage*?

I seem to be trying to thread my way between a lot of booby-traps. No wonder I'm ill at ease.

ST ALBANS COMMON

The road continues past St Albans, but you know you're leaving civilisation behind because after a few ks the bitumen falters, thins, and runs out into gravel. The First Branch bends away towards the west. Where it bends, a smaller stream called Mogo Creek joins it from the north, and the road follows it.

Back when the Wiseman boys were looking for land further north, this is the way they'd have come. That would have been about 1825 or 1826, so the pub wasn't built yet. Somewhere along Settlers Road they'd have passed the last farm. Then they'd have pushed on with their sheep into the unsettled lands.

At the junction where Mogo Creek joins the river there's a natural dam. Behind that dam a long, beautiful lagoon stretches away to the north, leading up through the valley so far that I can't see where it ends. There are reeds, and grass of that vividness and softness you only get with plenty of water. There are ducks and black swans. The breeze ruffles the surface, blue and bright. On either side trees rustle and sway, growing tall and thickly along the banks. This is one of those places – there aren't too many of them in our dry old land – that has a real Garden of Eden feel.

Where the lagoon starts, there's a sign beside the road. *St Albans Historic Common*, it says. *Private Property. Please enjoy travelling through our common and keep to the road at all times. Camping, shooting, fishing and picnics are not permitted.*

I'd been planning to stop, get out the thermos, unwrap a sandwich. No camping or shooting, okay – but no picnics? Really? Isn't the whole point of a *common* that it's common property – belonging to everyone? Isn't that one of those splendid old English traditions we admire so much?

I want to stop, and not only for a cup of tea. I want to see if something I'd been shown on one of those research trips is still here. I'm not sure I'll remember where it was, but as I grind along in first gear, the shape of the place suddenly lines up with my memory, and there it is! Just as it was twenty years ago, when I came here with a man who knew this place and showed me some of its forgotten marvels. In spite of the sign I stop and get out of the car, though uneasily, with the prickling *someone is watching me* feeling of a trespasser.

I'm looking at a huge old tree with a long scar in the bark where, a long time ago, a canoe was levered out. The tree has grown with a twist in its trunk, so the cigar-shaped scar is twisted too. It looks like a mistake, but Patrick explained that it was on purpose. A straight tube of bark has to be bent up somehow and sealed at each end to be useful. A curved tube holds its ends up out of the water. Of course!

Once you've seen it, you can't miss it. But before Patrick showed me that scar I'd driven past it several times, oblivious.

Twenty years ago I was full of admiration, a kind of exhilarated awe, at the ingenuity and economy of the design. I still feel that, but now the scar makes me aware of something else too – not a remote theoretical concept, but the actuality of Aboriginal people living here beside the lagoon. In this moment I imagine that I can almost see them and hear them, families going about their days in a place of ease and plenty. It's a spot where big groups of people could gather for special occasions, feasting on fish and eels, ducks and swans, wallabies and kangaroos and possums, and of course midyini.

As the foreigners moved up the valley, green bit by green bit, they'd have known about the people living beside the lagoon. They'd have called what was there a *camp*, a *blacks' camp*. That would fit with the way they liked to think about the people they were displacing: as nomads, like the gypsies they were familiar with back home. It was convenient to think of them as just passing through, *going walkabout*, with no fixed abode and no sense of being attached to a particular place. That was pretty much what I was taught, too. I believed it until I learned more. But the families who lived beside this generous lagoon couldn't have been mistaken for temporary visitors. They'd have looked – well, the word that comes to mind is *settled*.

I've been driving for quite a time, and the lagoon has narrowed into the creek that feeds it, when I come to another sign. It thanks me for visiting St Albans Common. I slow down, reread it. You mean the Common has only just ended? Surely it can't be that big!

When I look it up later, it turns out that the Common is gigantic. It's a long thin strip, 10 kilometres long and a kilometre wide, that starts at one end of the lagoon, where the dam is, and finishes at the other. It takes in every metre of the lagoon, straddling both banks and including the soft green strip on either side. The entire length of that wonderful body of water, and the rich land on its banks, is neatly enclosed within the straight lines drawn on the map.

It's there because in 1824, Governor Brisbane set aside an area "in such a situation as may best suit the interests of the settlers". What best suited the interests of the settlers, naturally, was to have the lagoon and the good land on either side of it. The settlers in the valley became joint owners of that common land. So, confusingly, the Common is actually private property.

It was nice of the governor to give that area to the settlers, but I'm wondering if there might have been an unspoken agenda as well. Once the settlers officially owned all that land, they'd have felt they were within their rights to treat anyone who came on it as a trespasser. From the governor's point of view it was rather neat. He didn't have to send soldiers out to protect the settlers. They could do it themselves.

They wanted the land and they were prepared to do whatever it took to get it. But they'd have been afraid, too. They were outnumbered. I'm imagining big meetings of Aboriginal people here in this plentiful place. The singing of many voices, the pulsing of many clapsticks. Fires large and small. Shouting and dogs barking and people dancing in the firelight, their bodies marked with white pipeclay. All normal social and spiritual business, but for the first white men here, sitting by their fires in the vast darkness of the nights, listening in ignorance of what the sounds meant, how easy for misunderstanding to turn into fear. So many *black natives*. So few *settlers*. Such a lonely and undefended corner of the Empire.

I don't think they'd have held back from *asserting their rights*.

Imagining the settlers by their fires, and Aboriginal people meeting and dancing, I'm feeling an immediacy, a concreteness, to the pictures I'm conjuring up. But of course I don't know any of this. This is just me, *imagining* and *conjuring up*, based on what I've learned from reading and listening. Imagining it so vividly feels like a kind of understanding, but is it really? It's one way into the question I set out with, but I have to remember that this is just me imagining, and not assume that's how it was.

This loose, open-ended process is the only way I seem able to approach the past and the puzzles that it creates for the present. The process is familiar to me, because it's a version of what I've always done in my novels. The difference is that this time I'm not using the screen of invented plot and characters. Today is just about me and the place, and I wouldn't be the first person to lose my way on someone else's land.

MOGO CREEK

Once I've left the Common behind, the country becomes drier and steeper and more uncompromising. There are no lagoons up here and none of those triangles of fertile land. Just the narrow V of the valley, and the stony hills rising steeply on both sides. Every slope is studded with great shelves and shards of the rock underneath, the pale bones of the planet bursting through. We colonists call land like this *inhospitable*. There's something a bit accusatory about it. It's as if we think the place is spitefully holding out on us.

That's why it's national park now. No one lives here, in all those hundreds of thousands of acres. But the people who retreated from Wiseman's place, the people who were pushed up the First Branch bend after bend, the people who were finally forced away from the greedy strip of the Common – they could have lived here. For a while, anyway.

This whole country was an intensely used landscape, even up on the stony heights, though these days it's hard to see the evidence. You have to be shown, as I've been shown a few of the marks left by those generations of life: engravings, their once-fresh gold now the same grey as the rest of the rock, so they're hard to find among the trees and leaf litter. Grinding grooves in the rocks. A cave with stencils made by spitting out a mouthful of clay-tinted water. There are outlines of boomerangs, and stone axes with their big rounded heads and short thick handles. I've seen the shape of a hand with a thumb bent like a hitchhiker's, another hand beside it with a kink in the middle finger, another that belonged to a child. I've put my own hand up to them, a greeting palm to palm across who knows how long.

But if you've ever been in bush like this, you know there's not that much food there. Yes, in their seasons there are birds and tubers and seeds. There are lizards and snakes. There are wallabies and possums and echidnas. Up there somewhere in that vast landscape above me there'd be small waterholes filled by the thready creeks that flow for a while after rain. If your family had been here for generations and generations you'd know where they were, and how to keep the water from evaporating. You'd know how to catch those wallabies and possums, know which roots and seeds were safe to eat. There'd have been spiritual knowledge of every mountain, every stream, every place of high flat rocks covered with engravings. For Aboriginal people this wasn't *wild*. It wasn't *inhospitable*. It would have been known and named, one of the many rooms in the mansion that was their Country.

Still, even for people who know what they're doing, and the meaning of the shape of every mountain, this wouldn't be a place you'd choose to live permanently. Over a long hot summer those waterholes dry up. The game is thin on the ground to start with because there's not much on these steep slopes for them to eat, and once you'd caught all the wallabies and possums within range, there'd be no more for a while. There's nowhere for midyini to grow.

You'd need to be able to move around a big area, and you'd need access to the places with good water and fertile soil, because for big gatherings you need a place that can feed a lot of people at once. If you were stopped from going onto the good land – well, you could eke out a living for a time, but I think it would be a hard and hungry one, and would slice across the networks of kin and kith that shaped your lives.

Kilometre by kilometre the road is becoming less assertive. It doesn't cut through corners or build itself up, but humbly follows every wiggle and coil of the creek. It's narrow, nothing more than a slot of level ground dug out of the slope that rises straight out of the creek bed. The car shudders over corrugations in the hard dirt and threatens to slide on the gravelly corners. I haven't passed another car since St Albans. If I slip off the road down into the creek I'll wait a long time for someone to come along and find me.

It feels as if this might always have been a road. In this dry stony landscape, among the mighty ridges and plateaus up above me, this narrow footing along the bank of the creek might have been the best way to get from the middle reaches of the Hawkesbury River to the rivers and valleys further north. Whenever people moved from one to the other, this is one of the routes they might have taken.

So when the Wiseman boys – my great-great-uncles – came along here, they mightn't have been bush-bashing, but tramping along a track that thousands of years of other feet had created. They'd have been on their horses, the dogs ranging up and down the sides of the track, pushing the flock of sheep ahead of them, and behind them the dray would have bumped along with all the things they'd need when they got to where they were going to *take up* land: flour and sugar and tea, axes and adzes and shovels, blankets and frying pans and shirts. Oh, and guns. They'd have been shouting to each other from horseback to horseback, swearing the way men like to swear, to add a bit of rhythm to some ordinary remark, and laughing, they'd have had running jokes, the way people do after a while, and they'd have turned their heads aside and spat to get the dust out of their mouths, and wiped their chins with the backs of their hands. The tumult of their passing would have gone on for quite a time. Afterwards there'd be a cloud of pale dust hanging over the track as the noise faded.

No one's watching me today, I don't think. But at the time the Wisemans pushed their sheep along this narrow track between the hillside and the creek bed, the landscape wasn't empty of people. Those men, my great-great-uncles, might have been watched. Whether they were or not, I think they might have *felt* watched. That's why I imagine the shouting and the swearing and the laughing filling the valley. They'd have heard the watchful silence. They'd have wanted to push it back.

Week by week there were more men coming along the track beside the creek, travelling through with their flocks and herds, their dogs and horses and bullock drays, every week more and more of them, tramping through the landscape as if they owned the place.

I want to get out and look at things but there's nowhere to pull over. I'd probably be perfectly safe leaving the car in the middle of the road, and something about being here makes me feel as if the rules don't apply. Still, obedient soul that I am, I grind on for a few more bends until finally there's a place where I can pull over.

As soon as I get out of the car I'm in a different world, one that operates on a different grammar. There are the bellbirds busily pinging away, one after the other, and hot dry air full of the hum of a million invisible insects.

It's beautiful, and it's familiar too, because I grew up in Sydney when there were still patches of this kind of bush to muck around in. And because it's full of memories and knowledge learned in childhood, I love it with the intimacy that comes of experience. When I decide to clamber up the slope – not far, I promise the sensible person inside me, this isn't a good place to get lost or break an ankle – I know how you do it. You don't grab those tufts of strong bladey grass, no matter how tempting they are when your feet start to slither away from under you on the loose stones. I know, from having done it so many times as a child, that they cut your hands as efficiently as a knife. I know about those bushes, that look soft but turn out to be so spikey they stab you right through your shirt. I know that you can't walk up slopes like these, you have to go on hands and knees, and you can't go straight up because above you is a maze of shelves and overhangs of stone, shelf after jutting shelf of sandstone. You have to keep peering up to see a way to weave up between them, and when you do you have to cling to your sense of what's earth and what's sky, because the hill looms above you so steeply that you feel it's going to fall on you.

It's been a while since I've done this. Quite quickly it's exhausting. I remember how soon you get thirsty in this place of dry, dry, dry, and the way the flies crowd in to drink your sweat, knowing you don't have a free hand to wave them away. When I get to a wide flat ledge of warm stone, I decide that's far enough. I haven't climbed very high, but already my car looks like a toy down there, the road a scratch of yellow dirt. Way below me, Mogo Creek is nothing more than a glitter here and there where a puddle is hanging on through this dry season.

I know that *mogo* means *stone axe*, and I'm assuming the creek was called that because it was a good place to grind an edge onto a stone axe. The flat ledges of fine-grained rock that the stream flows over in rainy times were natural whetstones. The axes ground here wouldn't have been made of local stone, because sandstone can't be ground to a sharp edge. The dense stone that would do the job would have come from landscapes with other geology, many kilometres away.

Come from – that's how I'm putting it to myself as I rehearse what I know about stone axes from books. A neat phrase, economical, neutral, relating more to geology and its variability than to human beings. That's my scrap of knowledge about stone axes, that I bring out so I can attach some understanding to the name of the place I'm looking at. I'm glad to know it. In fact, if I'm honest, I'm patting myself on the back for knowing it.

But sitting here on the warm rock that the place is made from, I realise that the way I'm putting it to myself – the story I've boiled down to a one-liner in my mind – is doing a good job of obscuring the picture. The stone wouldn't have *come* all by itself. It was *brought*. I can see that, in the eye of my mind: someone walking,

walking, walking, perhaps some vast distance, not just *bringing* the stone but *carrying* it, an actual weight in an actual human hand.

And now that I'm thinking beyond my first thought, I remember reading that the stone for axes was often *traded*, and I realise I don't have any image for *traded.* Trading means people organising supply and demand, doing the complicated dance of working out equivalence between, I don't know, a piece of stone and a lump of tree-gum? A piece of stone and a feed of oysters? Or a piece of stone as part of the arrangements for marrying the right woman to the right man? None of that has a concrete reality in my mind. There's been nothing about exactly how that happened in any of those books.

There'd be people who'd know exactly how that *trading* happened, although it could be a few generations since a piece of mogo-ready stone was carried here. It would be good to know more, but what I'm watching here is myself, a white person congratulating herself on knowing that *mogo* means *stone axe,* and that the stone had to *come from* somewhere else. I'm interested in how even a well-meaning white person like myself tells that story in words that let the actuality go vague and passive. I've got that bit of knowledge, but it's a weak little thing – old history, facts a person can rattle off – with no relation to real people in a real place. Sitting here on this warm rock listening to the leaves shifting above my head and feeling warm fragrant air coming up the hill, I'm thinking that bringing myself to the landscape was the right thing to do. There's knowing things, but when you're on the place, you can see how knowing doesn't get you very far.

Beyond the seam the creek has made in the land, unmeasured distances continue, valley after valley, ridge after ridge, as complicated and private as the enfoldings of a brain. Those ridges and gullies continue for a vast distance, covered with the small trees and bushes that somehow find a foothold in the stony soil.

Various words come to me: *magnificent*, *majestic*, *awe-inspiring*. But sitting on this rock platform, still puffing from clawing up the side of the body of this place, I know I can only feel that warm marvelling because I've got my bottle of water and my sandwich down there in the car. I stare out over the vastness, and the thing like fear that I'm feeling, and don't quite want to admit to, is what it would be like to be here in this landscape all by myself, a small bag of warm blood and soft flesh. Being here, thinking about the people who lived here for millennia before my lot arrived, and the way they knew their Country, makes me see how shallow-rooted my feelings for it really are, how ignorant my familiarity. In the great humming silence of this landscape – a silence created in part by what people like my forebears did – I know how little I really belong. I grew up an hour's drive away, but I have to accept that in a deep way, beyond mere familiarity, I'm still new here.

Back in the car, I'm driving into an immense solitude. The road winds on and on. At every turn there's another vista of trees and rocks. At some stage Mogo Creek veers off westwards and the road follows an even narrower groove, a crease in the land not named on my map, where water would flow only sometimes. The road is trending upwards now. Everything feels drier and the sky is bigger. It's wilder up here. There's a feeling of tremendous remoteness.

I still haven't seen another car and there are no farms, no sign at all of human life. Each bend of the creek opens up into another configuration of ridge and gully, endless variations on up and down, sunlight and shadow.

Something different seems to have happened geologically here. Each time I glance up to the skyline, what I see along the top of the steep hillside is a vertical cliff of pale rock, a kind of rim, like the rim of a pot. If you wanted to climb to the top from here, you'd be turned back by that implacable enclosing wall.

This is a landscape of tremendous power and presence. It's as if I came through Eden, back there at the Common, and now I'm into some sterner place. I'm finding I have to remind myself to breathe. I'm gripping the steering wheel very hard. I think I'm feeling a whisper of fear. Well, that seems appropriate. This is a landscape of a scale and gravitas that demands respect. A person coming into it without knowledge is wise to feel small.

BUCKETTY

I'm glad when the road takes on a purposeful, straight-ahead feeling. A short distance further and it meets two others: the now-abandoned Old Great North Road over the plateau I've just skirted, and the modern bitumen.

The Great North Road was a gigantic enterprise, an attempt at colonial mastery. It ran 200 kilometres from Sydney to the valley of the Hunter River, and it ignored the power of the landscape. Instead of easing itself through the shape of the place, as the road beside the creek does, it went more or less straight up the cliffs at Wisemans Ferry and speared across the dry plateau at the top. It was built by convict workers who laboured for years, building mighty buttresses and elaborate drains and bridges. The part between Wisemans Ferry and where I am now was abandoned almost as soon as it was opened. Now it's only used by hikers. People with flocks and herds preferred the longer but better-watered road I've travelled up.

Then steamships made the whole thing irrelevant.

The place where the three roads meet – some 40 ks north of St Albans – goes these days by the name of Bucketty. I've read that *Bucketty* is the Darkinjung word for *mountain springs.* Like so many Aboriginal languages, Darkinjung was nearly silenced in the nineteenth century by the coming of the foreigners, and it's now being revived from the records that remain. I'm wondering if something might have been lost in translation here – if *bucketty* is the word for *mountain springs*, it's quite a coincidence, since a spring is where you do things with buckets. I find myself idly speculating whether, rather than giving information about themselves and their place, the Darkinjung people might have been borrowing the word to turn it back on the foreigners. To remark on all that heaving and humping with buckets, men labouring and sweating to carry water from one place to another. Is it just to my ears that there's a whiff of mockery there that the foreigners might have missed, it not occurring to them that the Darkinjung could be laughing at them?

In any case, I'm having a break at Bucketty and while I have my cup of tea I'm looking at some bits of heritage stonework, part of the Old Great North Road. The road was beautifully done, every culvert and drain a masterpiece of fine stonework, and after nearly two hundred years they're still doing their jobs as perfectly as the day the convicts slotted together the carefully shaped stones.

The ruins and remnants are now a tourist attraction. They're enough like the mighty stone ruins of ancient Greece and Rome for us to understand and admire them. There's a penumbra of cultural associations, things learned at school and a million postcards of broken columns lying picturesquely in the grass and great stones levered upright. The equivalents in First Nations cultures – rock engravings, cave paintings, carved trees – tend to be hard to find unless you're shown. They might be sacred and hold secret meanings. Their history and significance are often obscure to us non-Indigenous people. All that makes it difficult for us to recognise that they're at least as profoundly meaningful and valuable as the relics familiar to us.

Beside a long curved wall of splendid masonry there's a picnic place with benches and an information board about the whole project, now called The Convict Trail. The board is quite excited about how important it all is.

> The convict trail is a reminder of the convict felons who built the road and made possible the financial success which followed settlement. The Great North Road is a national treasure of world significance.

Well, it's good to honour those unfortunate *convict felons* who had to labour under conditions of virtual slavery on this mighty and – at least on this stretch – pointless work. Good to remember that their brutal labour made other men rich. But *a national treasure of world significance*? That might be gilding the lily.

The other story here is about the way roads like this *made possible* the speedy dispossession of the First People, for whom *financial success* was an unknown concept. The board spares a thought for them too:

> The Darkinjung Aboriginals occupied this area north of the Hawkesbury River. They showed their tracks to white

> surveyors, explorers and adventurers, unaware of the catastrophic effects on their life-styles which would follow.

It's good that the sign acknowledges the Darkinjung people, and the damage. Still, there's something about it that makes me – in the mood this landscape has put me in – hear things in the words that I mightn't usually hear. I'm thinking, Would they really have *showed their tracks* to the foreigners? You read a lot about "native guides" in the early accounts of *exploration*, but was there more to it than Aboriginal people being helpful?

For starters, they mightn't always have needed to *show* their tracks. Those tracks weren't the erratic wanderings of beetles across the dust. Generations of Aboriginal people followed known and regular seasonal movements from place to place. Depending how often they were used and how many people used them, and how quickly the vegetation grew back, some of those tracks might have been obvious for anyone to see.

And if they weren't, why would the people show them to any foreigner who asked? Generous they might have been, but they were not uninformed. They'd have been in touch with their friends further south. They'd have been very far from *unaware* of what was happening everywhere the white men had come.

They might sometimes have shown the white men the tracks in order to steer them away from sacred or forbidden places, or to lead them off their country. Sometimes they were paid. And perhaps at times they *were* simply being helpful. But no matter exactly how it unfolded each time, I have a feeling it wasn't ever as simple as the white men asking and the Aboriginal people acquiescing. A judgement would have been made by them about how to respond, and a considered decision arrived at. But none of that thinking was part of the white men's understanding of what was happening when a "native guide" showed them the way. The sign's wording suggests that it's still not part of our thinking.

As for *life-styles* – if the reality wasn't so serious, the choice of that phrase would be funny. The *catastrophic effects* were a matter of life and death. They weren't about the Darkinjung people's fashion sense or their latte habits.

And behind all those words, as well-meaning as they are, is another message: that Aboriginal people were naive – that their lack of guile and awareness made them the agents of their own destruction. Quite a lot of blame is being quietly shifted here.

The board ends with a worthy enough sentiment: *All relics need care and understanding to go on stimulating the imagination of explorers like you*. Yes, relics do need to be cared for. But *explorers like you* – well, I can see what the writers of the sign were trying to do, but I have to object. Please don't call us *explorers*. That word implies that the place is a blank page waiting for history to be written on it. It wasn't true when the first *explorers* came here, and it isn't true now.

But of course, the sign has put its finger on the truth, and that's why I'm annoyed. I'm here because my ancestors *explored* this place. They came into it as if they thought it was empty, as if they were the first ones there, and they took it. That's the confronting fact, and it's why I'm here at Bucketty, deconstructing every word on a bland bit of signage.

Heading north from Bucketty, the bitumen carries you 10 ks down a mountain around a series of smooth bends and, quite suddenly, you're in the valley of Wollombi Brook. The Brook – what a Wordsworthian name for an Australian stream – starts as a series of small creeks, each one carrying a sliver of fertile green land, and each one has been given the name of the first foreigner to claim it: Fernance's, Murray's, Lynch's. As the valley runs north it opens out, with paddocks of clear land on either side of the stream. There are the same stony dry hills as further south, but lower now, hemming in the green rather than towering over it.

It's getting late, the sun winking through the trees on the top of the ridge. Time to turn up the side road to where I'm booked into a cottage at the back of someone's farm. I've paid in advance and the owners have explained they'll be away. *The key's under the mat, let yourself in. Enjoy!*

I can slip in, make a quick meal, and have an early night. I'm pleased to have found a place where I don't have to talk to anyone. I want to keep this mood going. Scribbles of thought and scribbles of feeling. I think that's what I'm here for.

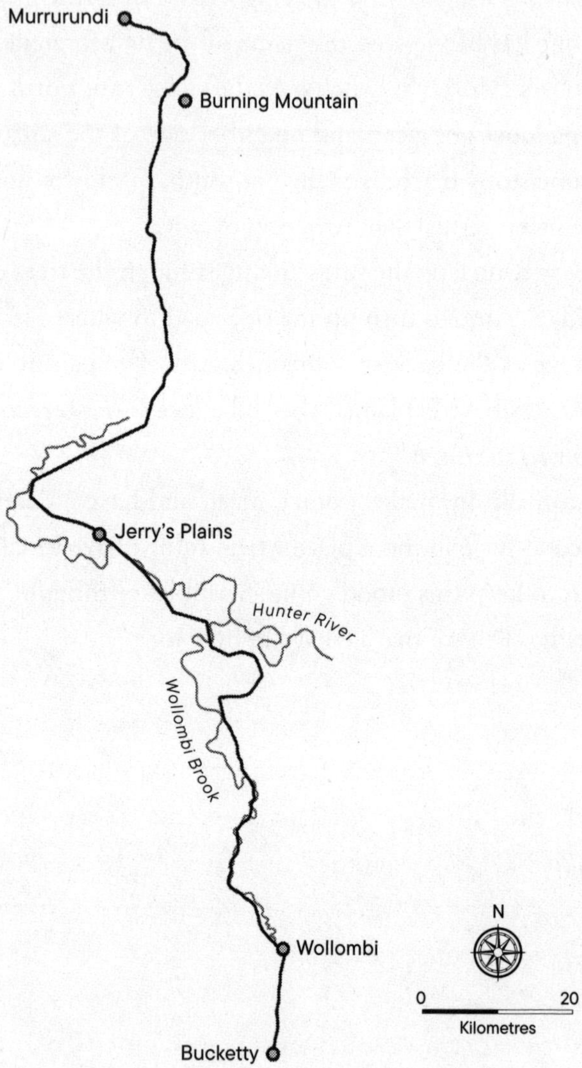
Murrurundi
Burning Mountain
Jerry's Plains
Hunter River
Wollombi Brook
Wollombi
Bucketty
N
0
20
Kilometres

WOLLOMBI

In the morning, after a deep and dreamless sleep, I drive along the valley in syrupy early sunlight. A sign tells me that Wollombi is supposed to mean *meeting place of the waters* in the language of the First People here. The *Bucketty* business is making me look twice at all these place names, and the thing about this one is that I don't see any *waters* actually *meeting* here. There's just the Wollombi Brook. But I know from my reading, and you can see from the place itself, that lots of *people* could have met here, where there was plenty of food and water. In which case, *meeting place* at *the waters* would actually make more sense.

It's only one little word. But as I look out over the lovely valley, long shadows across silvery-dewed grassy fields, I realise the big job that word is doing. Like the *up* in *took up*, it changes everything. *Meeting place of the waters* is about the waters. *Meeting place at the waters* is about the people. That's the bit we'd rather not look at.

And then, a few ks further on, I see I'm wrong – there *is* a meeting of waters here, where another stream joins the Wollombi Brook. There I was, thinking myself rather smart – and then the place itself sticks out its foot and trips me up. Yes, it's good that you're trying to see things in a new way. But don't get too full of yourself.

The Wiseman boys – Richard, Thomas and John – all set themselves up in various parts of this meeting place *of* or *at* the waters. Richard also opened an inn known as 'Young Wiseman's'. By the time he was twenty-one – in 1827 – the newspaper announced that he'd *already knocked up a temporary but comfortable house, with beds, and every convenience for the traveller* in the Wollombi valley.

Not without resistance, though. The newspaper reported that:

> The blacks at Hunter's river are again becoming troublesome to the settlers in this quarter. Mr. Wiseman jun. was surrounded a few days ago by a party of the blacks, ten in number, who forcibly took from him his jacket, in which were several orders for the payment of monies, and upon Mr. W's taking to his heels, they pursued him a considerable distance, but proving to be the more nimble footed, he succeeded in getting away.

Mr Wiseman Junior might have been *nimble footed*, but I'm wondering whether it really was happenstance that the jacket had IOUs in it. The *blacks* didn't have bank accounts, of course, but they might have known those pieces of paper were of value. Among the settlers (or their convict workers) there might have been some who'd exchange the IOUs for something Aboriginal people valued. The way I'm reading this is that they let Wiseman go because they had what they'd come for, and it mightn't just have been the jacket.

Of course that's speculation. But even to speculate is a reminder that the white people's side of the story is often the only one we hear. This newspaper piece doesn't consider the possibility that the *blacks* understood the value of those pieces of paper, and strategised to get them. The writer would probably have considered the idea absurd. The story is once again about the superior cleverness – or in this case the superior nimbleness – of the white man.

Richard isn't mentioned in my mother's story of our family, but Wollombi is:

> Solomon Wiseman had a number of children with his second wife, one of whom was called Sarah Catherine. She was my great-grandmother. She grew up near Wisemans Ferry in a little place called Wollombi.

The first bit of this is wrong – all Wiseman's children were from his first wife. I'd always assumed that Mum had the second bit wrong too. Why would Sarah Catherine grow up at Wollombi when her father lived at Wisemans Ferry? But I'd often doubted Mum's accounts and usually come to find them accurate.

Sarah was the youngest child. She was five when her mother died, pushed or fallen. A year later her father married again, and soon after that her brothers were heading north with their flocks.

The picture comes into focus: the little girl alone at home with the father and the stepmother. That mightn't have been much fun. As someone who's had a stepmother, I know a second wife doesn't always want the first wife's children around. I'm thinking now that Sarah might have gone to live with one of her brothers. Since all this is guesswork anyway, I'm going to assume it was Richard, with his *comfortable house with beds.*

The side of the valley is a series of spurs of land overlooking the stream, and Richard's inn was probably on one of those. Far enough up the slope to be out of reach of floods, but not so far as to be too steep to *knock up* a building. Before I came on this trip I'd made a few half-hearted efforts to find out exactly where Young Wiseman's was. I'd told myself I couldn't crack the land titles archive code, but actually I hadn't tried too hard. What difference would it make, which particular lovely rise of land Young Wiseman chose to knock up his inn? Wherever it was, it was a foreign footprint on someone else's country.

Now I wish I'd done my homework properly. The code isn't that hard, and the Archives office is full of helpful staff. Being here, seeing the way the land folds up and down along the side of the valley in such a beautiful soft way, there's a sense of having been too casual. Oh, it's just a bit of land, I'd thought. Does it make any difference whether it was *this* bit or *that* bit? Now I think, *yes*, it should make a difference to me, because it would have made a difference to the people who were here.

Even the half-hearted research I had done told me that Richard Wiseman eventually became one of the biggest landowners in the valley. On the old map you can see square after square, rectangle after rectangle, neatly labelled *RA Wiseman.* He bought most of them, but he started with a grant: 640 acres of prime land in this valley. It was given to him *in reward for [his] services in pointing out a line of road from Wiseman's Ferry to the Wollombi.*

I have a feeling he didn't have to do all that much to get his reward. There's not much water up on that plateau where the Old Great North Road runs, so there's really only one practicable route across it, and when Aboriginal people travelled up on the plateau they'd probably have used it. I think the route Richard Wiseman *pointed out* may well have been one of their tracks.

I've been hearing about *grants of land* ever since Social Studies in primary school. We learned about the place being *discovered,* and we learned about *explorers,* and we learned about *grants*, and I swallowed it all without thinking. Since then the work of historians has taught me to look twice or three times at those smooth words.

A *grant* is just a fancy word for a *gift.* The governor gave the land to whomever he wanted. He could do that because when Captain Cook *discovered* the country in 1770, his masters' instruction was *with the Consent of the Natives to take Possession ... in the name of the King of Great Britain. Or: if you find the Country uninhabited take Possession for His Majesty.*

Back then, I've learned, there was a set of legal fictions by which a colonising power could claim a place. You could say you were claiming it by *right of discovery*, by *right of conquest*, by *treaty*, by *purchase*, or by the fact that it was *terra nullius* – uninhabited, or without any form of government. They were nonsense reasons – it was never a level playing field between the colonisers and the original inhabitants – but they sounded good, especially when they were in Latin.

When he raised the British flag on Possession Island, Cook didn't actually say on what grounds he was claiming the entire east coast. He didn't get *consent* from anyone, and he knew perfectly well that it wasn't *uninhabited.* But he'd have been aware that his masters weren't especially interested in physically *possessing* a place unless it offered something of use to Britain, which this new place didn't seem to. The main agenda was to make a point to other colonising powers: *We're here first, so if anyone's ever going to do anything with it, it's going to be us.*

But a few years later, when Arthur Phillip, the first governor, was given his instructions, the place *was* suddenly looking useful, as a place to send criminals and as a strategic foothold in the Pacific. Phillip was appointed *Governor of our territory called New South Wales*, which had now been extended inland from the coast as far as the middle of South Australia. Without any legal basis ever being explicitly stated (*terra nullius* came later), this vast expanse – of which the British had only seen a few specks – was now, apparently, *our territory.*

Nothing was spelled out, so anything was possible, and even by the standards of the time, what happened here was extraordinary. In other colonies, the colonised people had a different sovereign imposed on them, but they were still considered owners of their land. Here, by a sort of sleight-of-hand, every square inch somehow became the property of the British king. Overnight and without fanfare, the entire enormous expanse became Crown Land.

The whole business had no real legal basis, but that reality was magicked away by a lot of legalistic patter. It started with the phrase *Crown Land*. *The Crown* was a dignified, impersonal abstraction screening the fact that the place was owned by an actual individual, a man called George William Frederick, or King George III. The bit of paper that gave the land away to other people was called a *Deed of Grant*, language that kept the solemn effect going. As did the thing called *quit-rent* – a token rent that the grantee paid the Crown. (Richard Wiseman's quit-rent was *a farthing a year for ever*.) That archaic bit of legal jiggery-pokery established a chain of ownership described as a *tenurial nexus*.

All those weird old obsolete phrases were kind of technical, kind of esoteric. They had the solidity of ancient mists-of-time law, as unchallengeable as gravity. But what that impressive, impervious structure stood on was the original unfounded assertion that the British king now owned half the continent.

The giving-away was carefully managed to maximise the chance of the colony making money for Britain. Land was given in small pieces to ex-convicts and ex-soldiers who looked as if they might turn into good farmers, and bigger pieces were given to free settlers if they had capital they'd invest in the place. It was also given as a reward to men prepared to *explore* the place, or in other ways *open it up*. When the governor signed that solemn bit of paper for Richard Alexander Wiseman, *640 acres*, and Wiseman took it and bowed, the two of them might have thought they were doing a graceful old minuet. But what they were really doing was a thieves' dance.

The Australian colony was one of very few in the world where settlement was done without any kind of formal arrangement. New

Zealand has the Treaty of Waitangi, and the American and Canadian colonists made a series of treaties with the different First Nations whose land they took. Treaties between colonists and First Nations were often unjust, sometimes dishonest and frequently ignored. They didn't always do much to protect the people with whom they were made. But they established a principle.

A treaty is often understood as a way for warring parties to make peace. That idea can be used as a pretext to reject the idea of treaty in this country – we're all Australians! We're not at war with each other! But a peace treaty is only one type of treaty. Beneath any kind of negotiated contract, including a treaty, is the principle that both parties are sovereign entities, entering as equals into an agreement. The very existence of a treaty acknowledges the status and rights of both parties.

A long-ago acknowledgement certainly isn't a clear path to agreement in the present, but it gives you a place to start. Any kind of negotiation can only begin by going back until you're able to find a place where both parties agree – common ground. From there you can go forward step by step. Even an unjust or dishonest treaty gives that common ground, because at the time when it was signed, the sovereignty of the colonised people was acknowledged – by both sides – and the need for negotiation recognised.

Here in Australia, we don't have anything that can serve us as that common starting point. No treaty was ever made. There was no acknowledgement of First Nations. There was no negotiating. All that's ever been offered is charity, to be given or withheld as non-Indigenous Australians see fit. Which is why, two centuries after the British landed, we're still trying to work out how to be here.

JERRY'S PLAINS

Men born in the colony, like Richard Wiseman, were known as *natives*. Of course the word means you're *native to* a place – you were born there. But when you read those old documents it's a bit startling to come across white people being referred to in this way. It's as if the new people weren't only appropriating the land. They were even appropriating the word they used for the people they were appropriating it from.

The *white natives* weren't nearly as far down the pecking order as the *black natives*. But they had a chip on their shoulder, because they knew they'd never be considered as good as someone born in the Mother Country. Worse than that, they were missing out on land. Richard Wiseman had to work for his modest grant (in theory, anyway) and the government had to come up with a reason to give it to him. But fresh-off-the-boat immigrants who had money and social status were being granted huge spreads.

John Martin Davis was the kind of man the white natives resented. He was from a well-to-do Anglo-Irish family and arrived in 1828 with a thousand pounds of capital and a letter of introduction to the governor. Straight away he was given 1280 acres – twice Richard Wiseman's grant – of prime land on the Hunter River near the village of Jerry's Plains, and free convict labour to work it. Davis's pale Irish skin wouldn't even have had time to get sunburnt before he came up there with a dray of necessaries and some convict workers and settled himself on his grant. He called it Mary Villa.

The Davises weren't what you might call real Irish – Catholic, Gaelic-speaking. They belonged to the Protestant Ascendancy, the British colonists who'd been given enormous swathes of Irish land over the preceding centuries and who now ruled the country. When it came to taking someone else's land, you could say the Davises had form.

I've seen the square drawn beside the Hunter River on the old map with *JM Davis* written on it in tiny neat letters, and I've read the Deed of Grant to that land in the Parish of Ravensworth. The old map shows a kind of bulge on the river near *JM Davis*, a big squarish loop, and lo and behold, there it is on the modern map, a perfect match. Written on the blank bit of green beside the river, there's his place, now called *Maryville*.

John Martin Davis was my great-great-grandfather. But where the family story is full of detail about my great-great-great-grandfather Solomon Wiseman, and bits and pieces about everyone else, it's remarkably silent about John Martin Davis. In the family story he's only a name. Every other thing I know about him I've found from research.

As I set out from Wollombi towards Maryville, some 75 ks to the north-west, I'm wondering, for the first time, why that's so. Why does he only have a walk-on part in the family stories, while the others have an aria? Is it because he was gentry, and the family preferred to think of itself as humble working-class? Or – I hadn't thought of this possibility until now, looking on the map at the place he *took up* – is there something about him beyond what I found in the written records, something that makes his story one you wouldn't feel like including in your family legend?

There's an odd unmoored feeling in being without any family stories for this part of the journey. That makes me realise how much I depend on them as a way to see what I'm looking at. The stories are a tin-opener to open the can of worms of the past. Without them, you might find a few facts and dates, but you've got no way to connect the past with yourself in the here and now, and think about what that means.

As I was doing the research about John Martin Davis, I chanced on an article about an Irish writer (real Irish, not Anglo-Irish) who took a traditional Gaelic story as her starting point. It was a story that belonged to her by right of birth, part of her deep connection to her country and its past, and she made it part of her imaginative work about herself in the present. As I read about her book I surprised myself by feeling a pang of envy – an actual physical thing, like a pang of hunger.

She had that dense richness behind her – centuries of stories that were part of who she was, stories that she could take up and connect to. What a gift, to be part of a shared world of ancient stories about the place where you belong. What an impoverishment, not to have it. How differently that absence must shape our sense of ourselves.

And here's the thing – the Gaelic poem is about the colonising British in Ireland – the John Martin Davis lot. It's about a greedy English magistrate who murders an Irish man because he wants his horse. Who wants to tell the magistrate's story, or count *him* as a forebear?

I'm starting to jot down the names of creeks I drive past. There'd be a story behind each one, an event fossilised in the name. *Two Mile Creek* – I suppose that tells you how far the *explorers* had travelled from some landmark when they reached it. *Breakfast Creek* – that must have been a memorable breakfast! *Frying Pan Creek* – did someone leave theirs behind when the drays rolled on, remembering only when it was too late?

And what happened here, that someone named this modest stream *Jump-Up Creek*? *Jump up* – that was Aboriginal English for *run away*, or – depending on what authority you're reading – *resurrection after death*. Either way, it's suggestive. Or *Accommodation Creek* – that was white English for *gunpoint diplomacy*. Somewhere up ahead of me is *Waterloo Creek*, as in, *They met their Waterloo*. Those names are traces, remnants, grim coded messages.

From Wollombi I'm heading towards that bulge on the Hunter River with *Maryville* written beside it. It's turned into a wet day, and I take it slowly along the rough narrow road through the hills. It's a journey that repays slowness. This is a stupendous landscape: in this weather the high interlocking spurs go back and back in every shade of grey, paler and paler into the distance. Looming dark masses of mountain half hide in the mist. It's not very often that you see the bush wreathed in gauzy drizzle, and its loveliness is so different from the stereotype of Australia that it opens a new way of seeing a familiar world. When I pull over and get out, it's very quiet. There's only the faint tinkling of Wollombi Brook finding its way between the rocks of its bed.

Then, around Broke, the dramatic wild glens are left behind and a domesticated, pretty place opens up, a gentle landscape with lots of nice ups and downs, the green of plentiful water, and smallish, human-scale farms with a few cattle, a few fruit trees, a paddock or two of grapevines. I pass stands of dark-trunked gums and handmade signs for *Stable Poo $4.*

Then I turn onto the highway and all at once it's awful. The clouds and mist have gone as if they'd never been. The sunlight is harsh and there are too many speeding utes tailgating me no matter how fast I go, the endless glitter of glare on cars and a sense of rush and aggression.

I'm suddenly overwhelmed with anxiety. What if the car breaks down? What if one of these utes carries through on its threat to go straight up my backside? Is my will up-to-date, and shouldn't I have burned a few more of my papers?

It takes me a while to understand that when I turned off that back road into the Hunter Valley, I'd turned into another country.

Back there was a tourist land, where the well-heeled from Sydney come for a weekend away in some sweet boutique place. The Hunter Valley used to be like that too – a place where you came for a treat, a weekend away in the country. But what I'm hurtling through now, with all the other cars hurtling along with me, is an industrial wasteland of coalmines. They're screened – sort of – by quick-growing casuarinas, so you only ever get the most fleeting glimpse. You can't quite believe what you've seen and you can't stop to check because there's nowhere to pull over.

Those glimpses are of devastation on a scale impossible to take in. Vast piles of purplish-grey dirt, long jumbly walls of heaped rocks, massive stepped ridges like ziggurats. Sheets of blowing dust cloud a pit too big to take in, a pit kilometres long, dry and ripped open with trucks speeding into it and out of it through earth laid bare as if flayed. Harsh grey light rains down on a stripped landscape.

Finally, to the blare of an angry horn behind me, I turn off the highway onto the smaller road that runs past Maryville. From the road I'm looking down a grassy slope to where the river must run behind a line of trees. On the other side of the river is one of those hellscapes, another piece of country that's been turned inside out, pulverised, chewed up and spat out as grey mullock.

Below a hump in the grassy slope I can see the roof of a house and a cluster of utes. I'd like to walk down there – is that Mary Villa? – but between me and the house there's a very well-maintained barbed-wire fence and a very locked gate. The utes down there don't look like a farmer's vehicles. They're more like the high-performance ones I've just been monstered by on the highway. I explain to myself why I don't need to climb over the gate and go down to the house and introduce myself to the owners of the many utes. I'm easily convinced.

The river flats are a brilliant green. To my Australian eyes, they're too bright, lurid and almost artificial-looking. I don't fancy them, but to John Martin Davis they'd have looked like home. And like wealth. He'd have ridden over his 1280 acres and seen wooded hillsides and, beside the river, spreads of grassland between big old trees. He might have thought, as so many of the early colonists are recorded as thinking, that the beautiful landscape spread out before him resembled nothing so much as *the park lands attached to a gentleman's residence in England*. It was land perfectly ready for a man to start farming. What a bit of luck, he'd have thought. How Providence is smiling on me!

He might have seen campfires sending up small smoke, huts, people moving about. To his eyes those men and women would have looked temporary. He'd have been told that the *black natives* didn't use the land productively.

Back in Mrs Linney's class at North Sydney Demonstration School, that's what I was told, too. Aboriginal people were *nomads*. They wandered, and if they saw some berries on their wanderings they'd gather them. If they happened to come across a kangaroo they'd hunt it. That was how they lived, on the happenstance bounty of Nature. It was incredible to me, because how could anyone find anything to eat among all those prickly plants that made up the bush? And how could you ever get close enough to a kangaroo to spear it? I admired Aboriginal people for being able to do it, but it was just one more way that they were incomprehensibly different from all the people I knew.

I know now that I was admiring them for the wrong reason.

Mrs Linney taught us that Aboriginal people *burned the grass to bring the game.* That wasn't wrong, but what they did wasn't simply a matter of putting a flame to some dry grass and waiting for the new growth. My understanding of what they actually did went through a profound shift when I read some of the literature of the last decade or so about Aboriginal land management.

What I learned was that the landscape John Davis salivated over wasn't the way it was because Nature had made it that way, but because Aboriginal people had. They'd curated and manipulated the landscape to encourage the plants that were their staple food, and to make hunting easier.

Anyone who's ever tried to creep close to a kangaroo or an emu knows how hard it is. They let you get up to a certain distance – about the distance a spear would be effective, probably – and then they bound away. Even the strongest hunter would have a hard time getting a regular supply of meat. What Aboriginal people did was to alter the landscape in radical ways to increase their odds of success. Using fire, they created a landscape-wide series of lures and traps. The lure was the patch of new grass. The trap was the edge where the grass ended in a place for a hunter to hide – undergrowth, or a hill, or rocks. An edge is what a hunter needs. The more edges there are, the more successful hunting is likely to be. Over thousands of years, precision burning had made great swathes of the country into a vast embroidery of patches and edges.

There's a painting by Joseph Lycett, one of the early colonists, that you could use as an instruction manual for the lure-and-trap idea. There's a strip of grass, with a kangaroo at full stretch, labouring up it towards a bigger clear patch on the top of the hill, where it thinks it will be safe. Behind it is thick smoke. It's been lured to the grassy patch at the foot of the hill and now it's being driven by the fire up the steep slope. It's confused and exhausted. On either side are tangled thickets of undergrowth where it can't easily travel. Up ahead are the hunters.

The other thing I've learned is that those great swathes of groomed land were divided up into territories. Each area was the responsibility, and the spiritual identity, of a particular group of people. The Country of one group wasn't marked by a boundary line of blazed trees or fences, and it might include a fluid zone shared by neighbours, but the boundaries were known, recognised and respected.

How is it that I know so much about the way ancient Egyptians managed their land (after all these years I can still remember the name for the bucket device they irrigated with – *shadouf*, there it is sitting in my memory, waiting to be accessed), but until recently I didn't have the faintest inkling of the brilliant way my own place was distributed among its people, and shaped and used?

By the time John Martin Davis arrived, First Nations people all over the country had created a landscape where hunting was relatively easy and plant food plentiful. They could live well, with minimal effort. Many of the early Europeans here – Captain Cook among them – noticed how little time Aboriginal people had to spend in food-gathering. He observed that they seemed to have plenty of leisure, and drew the parallel with the aristocrats of his own world. It was a very different experience for the foreigners. Without his dray full of supplies from Sydney and his animals from the other side of the planet, and his convict workers on the go from dawn to dusk, John Martin Davis would have starved on that same landscape.

When Davis stood, that first day, and looked down over his grant, the embroidery would have been laid out plain to the eye that could recognise it. But while hunters need edges, graziers need wide-open acres. You can't keep a flock together, or herd it, in a complicated landscape of grassy patches separated by banks of bush. Davis would have set about clearing the undergrowth and trees to give himself more open grazing land.

The unpicking of all those careful stitches probably didn't take long. To keep the pattern of edges functional, Aboriginal people had to burn small patches all the time, a kind of constant housework. But the coming of John Martin Davis and his sheep would have disrupted that here. It wouldn't have crossed his mind that the beautiful place he was looking at was as carefully and deliberately shaped as any of those *gentleman's parks*. And if it had, he'd have pushed the thought aside as ridiculous. It suited him too well to go along with the *nomad* idea.

Ever since I read the books that describe the lure-and-trap system, I've seen it – or think I have – on the landscape many times: strips up the side of a hill and odd bald domes of clear grass on the very top. I'm looking for something like that now – there's a hill behind me with scattered trees and a few bushes. Can I see any trace of meaning in the way the trees and bushes are growing? I want to, and maybe if I knew more I'd be able to. But I think this hill has been unpicked too thoroughly. The trees just seem to be scattered. There are no obvious clear patches or strips. The careful grooming of hundreds or thousands of years is gone from this hillside, as until recently it was gone from what people like me were taught about the past of our country.

All those times when I've looked at a hillside and thought I was looking at the lure-and-trap design laid out, I could very easily have been fooling myself. Still, when I look at a piece of country now, I'm trying to read it, to see meaning beyond its surface. My ability to read is at about the same level as my four-year-old grandson's – he's recently worked out that those squiggles on the paper mean something – but like him, I've now learned just enough to know there's something there to be read.

When I first understood how subtle, complex and ingenious First Nations land management was, I felt a kind of ground-dropping-away-from-under-my-feet shock. There was a sense of, *This changes everything*. Once it's sunk in how intensely the place was groomed and manipulated, how densely used, how carefully divided up into territories managed by different groups, it's impossible to hang onto that comfortable idea of *nomads* going *walkabout*. And without that, there's a kind of nakedness. There's nowhere to hide.

Davis was the first foreigner to *take up* that particular piece of land on the Hunter. How he interacted with the Wonnarua people is as unrecorded as how Solomon Wiseman interacted with the Dharug and Richard Wiseman with the Darkinjung. But there's enough on the wider historical record to show that when the Hunter Valley was first settled, it wasn't peaceful. The map tells you why. John

Martin Davis was granted that stretch of land in 1828, and by the time the map was drawn two years later every single yard of riverside land was part of a square with a white person's name on it. That wonderful groomed and fertile land was now forbidden to its owners.

Those owners naturally pushed back. Two years before Davis was given his land, there was a spate of deadly violence in the area, including a well-documented massacre of Aboriginal people near Ravensworth, just to the north of Davis's grant.

Violence was done by both sides, but it wasn't the same on both sides. Even limited attacks – some cattle speared, crops stolen or burned, settlers wounded or, rarely, killed – gave the colonists a pretext to respond, and when they did it was with disproportionate violence, of a scale and intensity that Aboriginal people couldn't equal. It was men on foot against men with guns on horses – settlers and their workers, but also troops of mounted and well-armed police.

We know now that there were monsters among the early settlers and police, sadists and psychopaths, people with no moral compass. There were also many – perhaps most – who did have a moral compass, but allowed it to be bent. In early Australia there were plenty of convenient compass-bending beliefs: the pseudo-science that said black people were inferior to white, the pseudo-piety that said black people were godless pagans, the pseudo-economics that said black people couldn't be thought of as owning the land because they didn't plough or herd. And there was the matter of space. New South Wales had so much of it. Couldn't the black people just go somewhere else?

Plus, stealing land was normal in the places they came from.

Solomon Wiseman would have known about the long slow theft called the *Enclosure Acts* in England. His son-in-law Thomas Crawford would have known about the blitzkrieg brutality of the Highland Clearances. John Martin Davis would have known that the land his father owned back in Ireland had been taken from Catholics. Whether you were a victim or a victor in the equation, taking land from other people was simply the way the world worked.

I'm watching myself think about the *Enclosure Acts* and the Highland Clearances, and I'm thinking, Oh, am I looking for a way to excuse John Martin Davis? No, none of that excuses what those early colonists did. It makes it worse. It shows why you can't dismiss frontier violence as a matter of a few bad apples and reassure yourself that your own forebear wouldn't have been one of them. It was about thousands of ordinary people willing to bend their moral compasses because it would benefit them, and because everyone else was doing it, and because they had all those rationalisations. Men like my great-great-grandfather could hide behind the pseudo-legality of what happened here. Hiding there, they could think their hands were clean. They didn't have to wrestle with moral dilemmas the way the great-great-granddaughter of one of them is doing.

There were honourable colonists. Newspapers of the time have letters from settlers deploring the violence and acknowledging that Aboriginal people were the *rightful proprietors of the soil.* Some settlers established relationships of respect with the First People, offering them refuge from the violence of other settlers and doing what they could to protect them.

But people with fully functioning moral compasses seem to have been in the minority. And in a way, those people point up more clearly what the rest were doing. The colonists had a choice. People they'd have known or heard about had come to different decisions about how to live on land they'd taken from someone else.

As for John Martin Davis, who knows where he sat on that continuum?

This road must be a shortcut for the mine workers and maybe it's the change of shift. As I stand by the fence gawping out into the glare, endless utes blast along the road. Some of them slow down to look at the old lady in her hat, her car parked skew-whiff on the side of the road, staring across at where the mine has reshaped the landscape. They probably think, Oh, a greenie working herself into a lather.

But actually, I'm kind of numb. I've been trying to whip up a bit of a frisson – *over there is where my great-great-grandfather lived!* But something about what's happening in this part of the country, the scale of it and the depth of the destruction, seems to silence thought and emotion. All I can say is that I'm overtaken by a tense, unhappy feeling that I'm in the wrong place at the wrong time in the wrong mood. And something about the ugliness and ruin here is making me lose faith in this whole project.

It seemed easy when I set off. I wanted to think about the family stories in the places where they happened, and somehow I had the idea that doing so would tell me what to do with the fact that wherever I put my feet, I'm on land that was taken from other people.

Being here, it's not so simple. For a start, the stories didn't happen on this ruined landscape. They happened on a landscape that's now impossible to stand on, one that's gone forever, no matter how much remediation happens. That's going to be the case wherever I go. We can't undo what was done – not to the landscape, and not to the people who lived on it. And there doesn't seem much value in perching on the high moral ground wringing my hands. My moral compass has the fine privilege of having had the dirty work done for it a hundred and fifty years ago.

It's not too late to pack it in and go home. After all, what did I think I'd achieve by doing this trip? *A pilgrimage*. That's starting to feel like a silly puffed-up bit of nonsense. Standing in this devastated place, and knowing that the horror we unleashed on the landscape is an all-too-vivid metaphor for the horror we unleashed on the people of the First Nations, it feels like an insult. No wonder I'm numb. No wonder I want to turn my back on it and go home.

A pilgrimage is supposed to be hard. It's supposed to be about something like atonement, even punishment. But it seems I'm not ready to knuckle down to anything like that. Instead, I'm getting cranky about people in utes, when after all they're just workers in a hurry to get home, and feeling outraged about the mines, when they're part of what makes my electrified life so comfortable.

It's confronting to be on this landscape. Thinking about the past and what to do about it has so far got me into nothing more productive than a dirty, sticky tangle. That question – *What do we do, now that we know*? needs to be asked. But maybe this journey isn't the right way to ask it.

I get in the car and go back down the hill towards the highway. At the intersection I'm dithering, flicking my indicator now left towards home, now right towards the next part of the story.

Another of the never-ending utes pulls up behind me. I sense a hand poised to give me a great blast on the horn. Without quite making a decision, I turn right.

MURRURUNDI

In the small world of that time and place, John Martin Davis would have known the Wiseman boys down the road at Wollombi. He wouldn't have been too gentlemanly to have a few drinks now and then at Richard Wiseman's inn. One way or another he met Richard's little sister, Sarah. By this time she was around eighteen. He was a gentleman and she was the illiterate daughter of an ex-convict, but she was young and female in a place without too many young females, and her father was wealthy and powerful. In 1834 they married and went to live at Maryville. A few years later they rented it out and moved to a farm called Glenmire, smaller but less isolated, at the town of Millfield.

Then in the 1840s there was a drought. Crops failed, stock starved, prices collapsed, and the end of transportation meant the end of free convict labour. Like hundreds of others, including his Wiseman brothers-in-law, John Martin Davis was declared bankrupt. In 1845 he lost Maryville, he lost Glenmire, and he lost all the cattle and sheep on those properties.

By 1845 he and Sarah had five daughters, the youngest a newborn, the oldest eight years old. They all headed north, and that's where the family story starts again.

> Sarah Wiseman married John Martin Davis and they started the hotel in Currabubula.

Now that I know what sort of things happened in the Hunter Valley when John Martin Davis was there, that sentence looks pretty thin. Those thirteen bland words are stretched over an awful lot of history.

I've been thinking I'll push straight on to Murrurundi, 100 ks north of Maryville. I'll spend the night there and decide whether to pull the plug on this whole trip. But on the way I see one of those brown signs that mean there's something significant: *Burning Mountain Walking Trail*. I'm feeling a bit shaky. I need a reset.

It's over a stile – what a modest but efficient way of keeping things in or out – and onto a trail winding up along the side of the mountain. The track goes up and up, threading itself through the trees. I'm setting off, but my heart isn't in it. Surely if Burning Mountain, whatever it is, was worth looking at, I'd have heard of it? And it's got nothing to do with the family story, so why am I wasting my time?

I'm hurrying up, glancing at my watch, calculating times and distances to Murrurundi. I've actually stopped and decided to turn back when, right on cue, a man comes down round the corner towards me with his two children. They all smile. I'm probably looking a bit frowny and puffed but I try to smile back. The man says, Oh, it's a fair hike, but it's worth the trip. Not too much further.

Something about the warm moment makes me decide to slog on, though I'm still unconvinced. Then I realise that out of nowhere, sliding up silently like a bit of stage backdrop from behind the hills, clouds have arranged themselves above me, and quite suddenly it's raining. Oh bugger, I've got no umbrella! No jacket! It feels like the last straw.

But it's a gentle, sweeping rain, the kind that doesn't last long, and it's coming down at an angle. I can see that all I've got to do is stand behind this big tree right here and I'll be dry. I stand pressed up against the bark and let the sweet rain fall around me. The softness of it, and the shelter the tree is giving me, feels somehow meaningful, as if my anxious, dogged planning and driving and worrying and brisk efficient walking are being invited to relax. Just stand here, cheek to cheek with this tree. The gathered-together clouds, the slanting rain, the tree, the small level patch for your feet behind it – it's all been done for you. You just have to stop and let it happen.

As quickly as it came, the rain passes, there's a small clear rainbow for a moment, and then the kookaburras start up, filling the hillside with their mad noise. There's nothing soft and sweet and sentimental about a couple of kookaburras giving voice. No: assertive, triumphant, proud. Maybe even mocking.

As I plod on up the track I feel something shift, the opening of a recognition: this is why I'm here. Not to get from A to B.

More than anything else, a pilgrimage is about going the distance. That's what I have to do. *All* I have to do. Go the distance and take what comes.

Finally I get to a place where the trees fall away and there's an open slope: the top of the mountain. There's very white dirt, and patches of reddish dirt, and slippages and fissures in the ground – the place looks as if it's been bulldozed. I feel a tremendous heat radiating out of the ground, and now I can see that, further up, there are actual wisps of smoke coming straight out of the white rocks, and I definitely don't want to go any closer.

Deep under the surface, a seam of coal has been burning for who knows how long. The colonists gave the mountain the banal name it goes by on the map, but it was burning long before they saw it. Standing there looking at the smoke drifting up from the invisible smoulder, it seems clear that this place of powerful, rather scary presence would always have been a site of story and meaning in Aboriginal cosmology.

What story, what meaning? Beyond the sketchy account on the tourist information board, I don't know, and that feels right. It's not my story, not my meaning, not my world. I don't have to go under the surface of this smoking mountain to know that there's a world there. Running alongside the known, the familiar, is difference. I don't want to erase it or try to make it mine. I don't need to understand or come up with answers to unanswerable questions. I just need to stand back, as I'm standing back from this burning fissure in the earth, with respect.

I'm thinking about that impulse to give up and go home. I'm

not usually such a quick quitter. Something was going on there, and I think it must be that I don't really want to know about the past of my family. I *think* I do, I *say* I do, I read the books and pore over the maps and squint at the old documents – but when you come right down to it, do I really want to think about the unfixable problem of being descended from colonists?

This possibly meaningless journey through the country of my forebears might not get me any closer to knowing how to be here. But I'm going to keep travelling, because something needs to be understood, and sitting at home at my desk isn't going to get me any further along.

Coming into Murrurundi it's a lovely landscape, with tree-covered hills and ridges among undulating paddocks. The country looks better the further north I drive – tidy white fences with horses behind them, a sense that the place is lived in and loved. Well, not everywhere – there's a lumpy paddock with a tumbledown house that seems to be running away from the long tail of inchoate country rubbish streaming out behind it.

I've booked a place online that turns out to be a good choice – it's an old railway carriage that's been turned into a cabin. The old-fashioned curved roof, made out of strips of wood, makes the space cosy and cocoon-like. As I'm drifting to sleep I can hear the rain again, a soft, comforting backdrop to dreamless sleep.

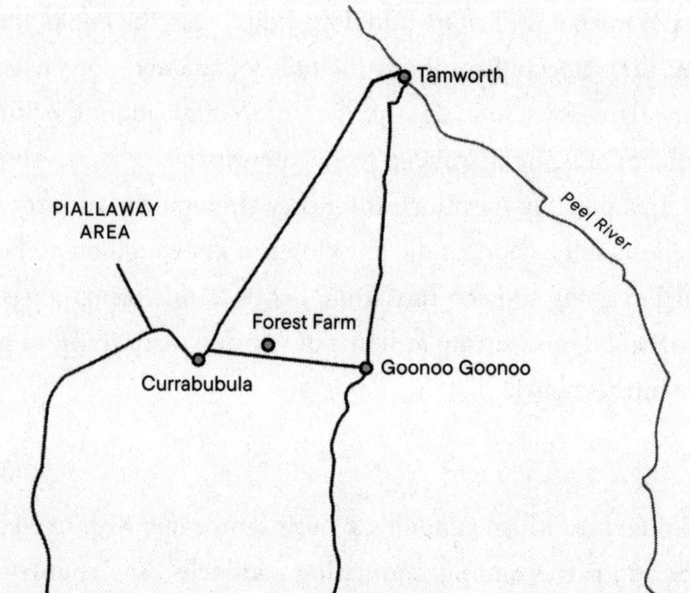

Tamworth
Peel River
PIALLAWAY AREA
Forest Farm
Currabubula
Goonoo Goonoo
Lindsay's Gap
Quirindi
Wallabadah
Murrurundi
N
0
10
Kilometres

CURRABUBULA

As soon as you leave Murrurundi the road suddenly tilts upwards into high ridges dark with bush that mount up one after the other. There's a sense of leaving a world behind as you start to climb the range, and in a way you are, because this is where, in 1826, Governor Darling declared that the "settled districts" ended. He drew a gigantic semi-circle on the map that showed the *limits of location* – beyond that imaginary line, the Crown hadn't actually *located* by survey any particular bit of it on a map. The King might have thought he owned it all, but he didn't have a clue exactly what he owned.

Whatever it was, the governor didn't want people going there. The colony was still a jail, and out there on those unmeasured vastnesses it was too difficult for the authorities to keep control.

The road climbs, then flattens, then climbs again in a steep, long, curving piercing of the mountains that have been ahead of me in the distance all the way up the valley of the Hunter River. My ears are popping as I climb. You couldn't have missed the fact that you were breaching a boundary, going beyond what was legal. You wouldn't need a sign or a fence. The topography itself carried the message.

At the very top of this steep passage there's a fork in the road. To the right is the most direct route north. To the left is the longer way, through Quirindi and Werris Creek to Currabubula, 70 ks north of Murrurundi. That's where I'm heading now.

Up here on the top of the range it's a different climate, a different world. No more lush green paddocks with pampered horses, no more winding and climbing through peaks. This is flatter country, tougher and dryer. It's broad-acre grazing country. You have to be prepared for distance here, settle yourself in for the long haul.

On my right, to the east, a high ridge presses in, a rough mass of rock, thinly clothed in dry scrubby bush, that runs beside me like a wall, on and on. To the west a pale plain shimmers into the distance, with scattered trees, cattle clustered under them, and golden grass. Those miles and miles of flatness out there to the west – you think, How vast. There's so much land. Thousands and thousands of acres, a sense of an inexhaustible supply.

I'm half hypnotised by distance when I see up ahead that the high ridge on my right has a bend in it, like a finger pushing at a string of beads. Where the bend makes the range crooked, you can see there's an opening. Here, as nowhere to north or south of it, you can cut through from one side to the other.

The first recorded white person to see that bend and the creek that runs through it was Thomas Mitchell in 1831. Like the other *explorers*, he was looking for land where people like him could run animals and grow crops. He was the advance party for the great colonial project of extracting value from other people's country.

The Gomeroi people would probably have known about him for days, messages travelling up ahead of him as he trundled obliviously through the landscape with his horses and bullock drays. They might have been waiting for him, out of sight but watching, when he got to the creek. The logic of the landscape said that he'd be likely to stop there, where there was good water after a long dry stretch, grass for the animals and shelter from the wind.

Here's how he describes it in his journal:

> The most conspicuous hill of those on our right was named by the native "Barragundy" … We at length entered upon an open and grassy plain, and found in the skirts of the wood beyond it a channel containing water in abundance, and which was known to the natives as "Carrabobbila".

I'm trying to imagine that afternoon: wood being gathered, campfires lit, tents erected, pots and kettles put to steam on the fire. At some point a few Gomeroi people must have approached and I imagine that *the native* (Mitchell's guide) spoke to them. Mitchell would have stepped forward and probably offered a gift – tobacco or something made of metal, a knife or tomahawk. I think he'd have been smart enough not to insult them by giving them beads and mirrors. None of that detail is in the account he left of that day, but he learned what he thought was the name of the place. He made the small black marks in his notebook: *Carrabobbila.* Some say it means *two-forked tree*, meaning the place where two ranges meet. Others say it means *spring of water*. Both describe the place.

Here's how Currabubula comes into the family story:

> Sarah Wiseman married John Martin Davis and they started the hotel in Currabubula. When the Davis family finally sold the hotel they'd been there continuously for a hundred years. Strangely enough, when it was eventually sold, a man called B. Davis bought it.

Continuously for a hundred years! In an Australian family story, that's forever. Well – a non-Indigenous family story, that is.

When Mum said that, she wasn't quite boasting, but she was telling me that it was something to be proud of. It meant we'd been here, in Australia, for longer than most people we knew. In a country where, according to the history books I grew up with, history started in 1788, going back a hundred years gave you a certain standing. And that coincidence – *Fancy, a man called Davis bought it!* – gives the whole endeavour a cheerful sort of feel, something like an endorsement from the gods of chance.

And they started the hotel in Currabubula. That's very matter-of-fact, and it sounds sensible. This spot beside Currabubula Creek was an obvious place for a pub. It was on the track that continued north to the Peel River and beyond, and in the 1830s and '40s there were plenty of people making that journey – ambitious men with flocks and herds, ignoring the limits of location. They needed food and water for themselves and their animals. I'd always thought the Davises had a nose for business, saw there'd be good money in a pub here.

What sort of man was John Martin Davis? No idea. Nothing

in my research gave any clue. But I'd always been glad that he was a publican rather than one of the men who ran sheep and cattle on big spreads out here in the backblocks: the squatters.

At school we'd learned that the wide-open spaces of the country had been settled by *squatters*. Many old squatting families now prefer to call themselves *pastoralists*, and I suppose that's because *squatter* is a double-edged word: a squatter is a person illegally occupying a place, and squatting is an undignified sort of thing, with the suggestion of going behind a bush to do your business. On the other hand, in Australia the word also signifies old money, privilege, gracious nineteenth-century homesteads covered with wisteria. There it is in "Waltzing Matilda": *Up came the squatter, mounted on his thoroughbred.* It's why these days the old squatting families are sometimes mockingly called *the squattocracy.*

The thing about squatters, and the reason I'd been glad I wasn't descended from one, is that it was the squatters, out beyond the limits of location, who did some of the worst of the violence in the early days. There was plenty of violence within the "settled areas" too, but the military were often involved, giving it a veneer of officialdom and legitimacy. But beyond the settled areas that veneer – the Border Police and the infamous Native Police – ran pretty thin, and even those official groups were beyond the close scrutiny of the authorities, and were free to commit whatever violence they were inclined to.

But out in the remote parts, much of the violence was done by the men who'd taken a big chunk of land and were willing to do whatever it took to hang onto it. They were confident that they could act with impunity – distance was their protection. There was shooting, men with rifles on horses. There was poisoning, bags of flour laced with arsenic or strychnine. There were killings of warriors, but there were also killings of women and children and old people. There were killings one-by-one, and there were massacres.

Very little of all that was ever written down, for obvious reasons. But thanks to patient and painstaking work by historians, who have unearthed what written records still exist, there's no longer any way to deny that those things happened.

The best-documented and best-known of the killings is the Myall Creek massacre in 1838, when around thirty Aboriginal people were killed in cold blood. We know some detail about that because, very unusually, the white men who committed the murders were brought to trial. Seven white men were hanged, and as a result other men were more careful. The violence didn't stop, but it went underground.

But a man with a pub wasn't in naked competition with Aboriginal people over land, the way squatters were. His footprint was small, and he wasn't running sheep or cattle that competed with the way the Aboriginal people used the land. As I'd learned more about what had happened on the frontier, I'd taken some comfort in that. I've always told myself, At least he wasn't one of the squatters.

Along with Wisemans Ferry, Currabubula is the other place where I'd spent a lot of time on earlier research trips. The times I went to Wisemans Ferry were for the novel based on Solomon Wiseman. A few years later I was researching for a book about my mother. Her mother had been distant and not especially loving, and had sent her to live for long periods with an aunt in Currabubula. It worked out well – Auntie Rose gave Mum the love she didn't get from her mother. I'd visited the school Mum had gone to here, found what I thought might be Rose Cottage, where she lived with that aunt, had a look at the hotel owned by her Davis cousins, and mooched around trying to imagine my mother as an eight-year-old.

There's not much to Curra. Half-a-dozen streets with modest houses, a petrol station doubling as the village store, a school, a closed post office. To the north there's the mountain called Duri, as perfectly cone-shaped as the sand in the bottom of an hourglass, and to the south – part of that long ridge that ran beside me all the way from Quirindi – there's a lumpy, shadowed heap of bush topped with raggy rocks. This is the landmark that Mitchell recorded as "Barragundy". Its official name is now "Warrigundi" but locals call it Terrible Billy. One version of the name's origin is that it's the mangling by English mouths of Carrabobbila. Another version says it's named after a stockman called Billy who did terrible things.

The village is nearly a pretty place. Currabubula Creek flows around the edge of it, but the buildings all turn their backs to the creek, and the old shape of the village has been made ugly by a new highway carving across the logic of creek and community. Wedged into the bend in the range, the village struck me on that first trip as a sad place with a shellshocked air, the few old houses on their few old streets marooned between lengths of bitumen, as if something had been broken apart.

The hotel was for sale then, a half-ruined place with brickdust crunching underfoot and dark green paint peeling off the walls in continent-shaped shards. Up on the parapet the words DAVIS HOTEL were spelled out in concrete. Davis had done well enough to own most of Currabubula by the time he died, but a hundred years later his proudly named hotel seemed to be crumbling back into the dirt it had come from.

The hotel is still the first thing you see as you come to the village from the south, and in fact, till you get closer, it looks as though it's the only structure for miles around. It's a gaunt brick building along classic Australian country pub lines: two storeys, a wide upstairs verandah with iron lace, a high roof, tall chimneys. It's incongruous, standing seemingly alone in a landscape of rolling paddocks and bush-covered hills. This pub isn't the original building, of course, though it's on the same spot. The first building, known as Paddy's Inn, would have been a crouching sort of place with a dirt floor.

A decade after I was here on that earlier trip, the pub's been renovated and it's Under New Management. It's called the Currabubula Hotel now and I notice that someone's chipped off the concrete DAVIS HOTEL. It's been nicely done out in the heritage style: fresh paint in muted old colours, a big mahogany sideboard in the foyer, antique light fittings, framed pages from old newspapers up on the walls. I glimpse a headline: "Thunderbolt Robs Davis Hotel".

I go into the bar and order a lime and bitters. I'm not thirsty, but I want something here, though I don't know quite what. Well, let's be honest – I want it to be known that I've got a connection to the place. I'm descended from the Davis who started it, whose name used to be up there in concrete. I'm not a clueless blow-in from the city! I belong here!

The woman behind the bar has the look of being the owner, so, leading around to the conversation I seem to want to have, I ask, Have you had the place long?

Three years next month, she says. She waits, looking away. I feel as if she thinks I might be a spy from the tax department. It might have been the wrong thing to lead with.

Only, my great-great-grandfather started it, I say. John Martin Davis.

She glances at me now, and I watch her register what sort of person she's dealing with: grey hair, no makeup, worn jeans. Ah, an old chook after her family history.

Oh well, she says, yes, we've got some information over there – gesturing at some more dense newsprint in a frame. I go and peer at a piece about John Martin Davis riding all the way to Maitland to apply for a liquor licence. I wouldn't have thought you'd have had to be that pernickety about such a thing back then, not way out here. So can I flesh out the picture of John Davis – Irish enough to be called Paddy, smart enough to see the potential of this spot, and – here's a surprise – a stickler for the rules?

The owner's come out from behind the bar and joins me looking at the newspaper. She tells me what she knows about the place. Davis was married to Sarah Wiseman, she was the daughter of a convict, they named Wisemans Ferry after him. Davis was from Ireland, the pub was called Paddy's Inn at one stage.

Something is making me awkward. I wish I hadn't come in. It's not her fault – the awkwardness is all mine. It's the fact that I feel a kind of ownership towards the place. Maybe not ownership but definitely a connection. And I'm unhappy that it's not being acknowledged. She doesn't have that connection. For her, my great-great-grandfather is just a bit of antique decoration to put up on the wall. She's telling me the stories that are mine – my own family, my own stories!

But how ridiculous to feel so affronted. She's got at least as much right to those stories as I have. After all, she lives here and I don't, and she's restored the hotel to something like its former glory. She knows the stories and she's showing respect to them and the people they're about. And here I am, getting myself into a tangle trying to work out whether I should feel what I'm feeling.

Outside the pub I get in the car and start the engine, but I'm not ready to leave. I have a longing to get away from Currabubula, the village made by my forebears, and get back somehow to Carrabobbila, the place that was here before. And that starts with the creek, only a few metres away. I can't see it, because it's hidden in a deep cleft behind the pub, but I know it's there.

Between me and the creek there are various tumbledown sheds and a fence, but there's no gate. If I want to get to the creek without going through the pub, I'm going to have to slide between the wires of the fence. It'll be obvious that I'm doing something the fence is telling me not to do. But what the hell, John and Sarah Davis were my great-great-grandparents. I've got a right to dabble my fingers in the creek! The old sheds aren't really old enough to be interesting – they're not *heritage* – but I decide that if anyone challenges me, I'll tell them I'm doing a study. *Assessing vernacular rural structures.* That should do the job.

How easily I slip into the frame of mind of a trespasser.

Quickly, quickly, I slide between the wires and take the few steps to where the ground falls away into a deep gully the water's made. I slither down and there at last, running sweet and sparkling over rocks and gravel, is the shining water.

No one can see me. Still, I feel watched. Why this heart-beating-fast feeling, this cranky readiness to fire up at anyone who questions my right to be here? All I'm doing is standing in this other country of tinkling water and rustling she-oaks, thinking about how the mystery of the past is embedded in a place.

I'm face-to-face with the sliced-off bank, a couple of metres of dirt and pebbles laid down by floods and cut through again by the swift little stream. And there, near the top where my hand can easily reach it, a shard of old blue-and-white dinner-plate winks out at me, exposed like a dinosaur fossil by the action of the water carving away the bank. Is this a bit of a plate that long-ago Sarah Davis ate off, washed, dried with a tea-towel and put in a dresser? That one of the children dropped one day and got a clout over the head for, and the broken bits were thrown down beside the creek with the rest of the rubbish?

I smooth the old glaze, clearing off the dirt, and the movement of my thumb over the pattern makes me think of Mum. When she lived in Currabubula as a child she had a cubby, she'd told me, and in the cubby she had a collection of chainies. Chainies? I'd asked, What are they? She'd laughed. Oh, it's just what we called them, she said, I don't know why. Little broken bits of plates, broken cups, things like that. Why are they called chainies, I asked, but she was smiling at her memory and shook her head. She didn't know.

It wasn't until I went to Ireland years later that I got the answer. The taxi driver who was taking me to a reading was one of those who like to have a conversation, and we got talking about the Chinese. Investment, perhaps – it was during the Celtic Tiger times. Oh, yes, the Chinese, he said. His Irish accent was strong, and in his mouth there it was: *chainies.*

It's how my mother's great-grandfather, John Martin Davis from Cork, would have spoken of the plates and cups on his table. His daughter Sarah would have learned that way of saying it from him and passed it on to her daughter. That daughter – my grandmother – would have passed it on to her daughter, my mother. And there I was, standing beside Currabubula Creek hearing the Irish in my own mouth as I whispered the word.

Chainies are everything and nothing. Concrete and real and robust, the glaze still dark after how many years, but also lost, a floating speck of the past that can be attached to anything. It can set you dreaming, and it can remind you of the humble physical reality of the past. Even if Sarah Davis hadn't owned the plate this fragment was from, even if it wasn't one my mother had in her cubby, it had been used by people far in the past. I was wandering around in Currabubula looking for something that was no longer here, but the chainie was telling me that the past had once been as real as my today. Telling me that my mouth, formed in part by generations of Irish genes, could remember the sounds of that other place, as if, just for the moment I was saying the word, I was still Irish. Not a foreigner, but only a few degrees of separation from being one.

PIALLAWAY

In the National Museum of Australia there's a collection of things from the nineteenth century called king plates. They're big crescents of brass with a loop of light chain attached so they can be worn around a person's neck. A person – well, an Aboriginal person. The idea was, a white person got one of these brass crescents made and had it engraved, usually with the name of someone he thought was a local leader, such as "King Billy, King of the Barwon Blacks". Sometimes they were presented as a reward for service, or even for being "the last" of their "tribe". Most were presented to men but a few were given to women. Some were given by the governor or other officials, but many were presented by squatters out on the big runs. Some included images: a kangaroo and emu, like a coat of arms, or leaves and flowers. Others were etched with lines that were supposed to match the pattern of ceremonial scars on the recipient's body. In the case of king plates given by squatters, the name of the run was often engraved too.

Some king plates recognised people of genuine authority within their community, but other people appointed "king" by the colonists had no special status with their own people. Whoever they were given to, and whatever the ostensible reason, the rewarding or honouring of certain individuals above others was part of the colonial calculation: how best to dominate and render harmless the people whose land they were taking. It's a trick as old as colonialism – to buy off, or ingratiate yourself with, someone you think might influence the others.

Looked at that way, the king plates were an insult wrapped in an honour. An honour, because what could be better than being a king? But an insult, because there was a mockery to the white men calling an Aboriginal man a king. They didn't think of any of the Aboriginal men as equal to a king, not for a moment. And their own kings, in red velvet and silver ermine, wouldn't have been seen dead in one of these clumsy brass things. More insulting was the assumption that the authority Aboriginal leaders had needed confirmation from a white man. The deepest insult of all was that the person presenting the plate thought that the person receiving it would feel flattered.

It seems that some of the king plates were given in a spirit of genuine respect, and that some recipients were proud to wear theirs. But other recipients, in other circumstances, might have done a different sort of calculation. They might have formed the view that, if the white men thought you'd been bought off, they might be less likely to kill you. The king plate would be worth accepting because it might function as a kind of safe pass among whites.

There are photographs of men wearing the king plates. They stare at the camera, their faces unreadable. The way I'm imagining it is that, if saving yourself and your kin depended on pretending you were flattered by a bit of brass round your neck, you'd do it. But you wouldn't pretend to be pleased.

I'd been doodling around yet again on Google one day, looking for more information about John Martin Davis, when I came across something newly uploaded – an article on the Museum of Australia website about those king plates. According to the article, John Martin Davis had presented one to an Aboriginal man. The evidence is flimsy – a throwaway line in a much-later newspaper – but Davis was in the right place at the right time. The crescent is engraved "Mr Briney of Piallaway". No one knows who "Mr Briney" was, or why he was given that name, but Piallaway isn't far from Currabubula, and the museum is prepared to believe that John Martin Davis presented this thing to him.

You could invent a story about Davis, the honourable settler, coming to an accommodation with the local people. Davis sitting down with Mr Briney and presenting him with that crescent of brass. Going through the motions of, I don't know, negotiation and compromise, amity and kindness?

Well, that's a pretty picture, and it would be comforting to believe it. But I don't. The very existence of the king plate suggests that there was conflict. If John Martin Davis gave one of them to a local man, he was probably trying to buy peace. Who'd go through the pantomime of presenting the brass thing to someone, if there wasn't an urgent need to get him or her on side?

I found all sorts of reasons to procrastinate, but one day I typed *John Martin Davis Piallaway* into the National Library of Australia's Trove search box. Trove supplied the newspaper account of a trial that took place in 1856. It was a dispute between two squatters about where the boundaries of their lands were. Both pieces of land were in the big general area called Piallaway, a few miles north-west of Currabubula. John Martin Davis was called as a witness because he was a neighbour of the plaintiff and could therefore give evidence about where the boundaries had originally been. He told the court that he *went up to Piallaway in 1832. His station was between two arms of the range, to the end of Spring Creek, with McDougall's to the west.*

There's no sound when something shifts in your sense of yourself. You don't cry out. For a while there's not even any feeling. It's like when you cut yourself – it takes a moment before you register that your snug package of skin has been broached. That's how it was when I discovered that my great-great-grandfather didn't just have an inn. I'm not descended from some jovial mine host, keeping his hands clean on a dirty frontier. My great-great-grandfather was a publican, yes. But he was also a squatter.

What the squatters did to claim their vast runs was shockingly simple. This is the way Davis's neighbour Andrew McDougall described how he came by the piece of land in dispute. He and his brothers came up from Sydney in 1832, he said, and *No stations were then marked out but all was an open space before them. They chose the run in question and had held possession ever since.*

There was no mucking around with surveyors or maps. There *were* no surveyors or maps out there beyond the limits of location. The Liverpool Plains – of which Piallaway is a part – was beautiful country, but it was called *Waste Crown Land* – meaning land the Crown had no immediate use for. All you needed to *hold possession* was a flock of sheep or a herd of cattle. The extent of your land was pretty much just the distance your stock could forage from the hut. The more stock you had, the more land you could call yours.

When Davis claimed his *station* in 1832, he was still living at Maryville. The way I'm picturing it is that he went up to Piallaway with someone who knew the bush – possibly a man called Dennis McCarthy, who later managed the Piallaway run for him. Once they'd picked out the run, Davis went back down to Maryville and went on living there, using the Piallaway land as another place to run his stock. Then some time later – perhaps when he was bankrupted – he and his family came north and set themselves up at Piallaway.

However it happened, exactly, what I have to accept is that he had the land at Piallaway before he had the pub. He still had the land when he died in 1866. There's no fudging it. He was a squatter, all right.

This is my mother's story about the Davis generation of the family:

> Old Granny Davis, as my mother called her – she was my mother's grandmother – lived there at the hotel and lived to be ninety or so. She was blind in her later years and was renowned for her stories.

> Granny Davis had a lot of stories about "the blacks", as they called them then. All the stories I ever heard, they were always "the blacks". "The blacks" did this that and the other. And of course, there was never a good word for them. The stories would be, you know, how "the blacks" would come down and no woman would ever be left in the house without a gun. There were lots of stories about women going out and – I don't know if they actually shot any of them, but they'd go out with the gun and show "the blacks" that they had it.

I'd listened to Mum tell me this dozens of times as I grew up. She'd told it to me, she'd written it down in her notes about the family history, and she'd even spoken it into a tape recorder when I asked her to. But somehow, I'd never let myself actually hear what it was saying. I'd only taken in the bit about Davis and the pub, and my picture of him was as that cheerful publican modestly compressing his footprint to no more than what he needed to run a pub. It was only after I followed the king plate lead that I was prepared to hear the other part of the story. What those few sentences from Mum hint at is shocking. But in a way, even more shocking is that for my whole life I knew it, but blanked it out of the picture of my family's past.

Now that I seem ready to hear the truth, I can see how easy the story made it for me to not-quite hear it. How muffled it is, how evasive. The stories about Wiseman were crisp with certainty, even when they were wrong. But this is a thin insipid little thing.

Partly it's that there are too many voices. There's Granny Davis, telling her stories, and there's my grandmother, telling them again. Now my mother's telling them to me. And she's putting herself into the story. You can hear her at every turn, editing what she's heard as she re-tells it. What you can hear is that she's uncomfortable.

In Granny Davis's day, conflict with Aboriginal people was commonplace. She was probably living with her brother Richard when *the blacks* made off with his jacket and all those IOUs. There'd have been plenty of talk among the settlers about how to deal with the *troublesome blacks*, and it's safe to assume there was retaliation against them. Violence reported in those early days was very often spoken of lightly, even in a jocular way. In the worst accounts, on the more remote edges of settlement, it was portrayed as something like a fine day's hunting.

But by the time Mum was telling me the stories – in the 1960s and '70s and '80s – things had changed. Violence against Aboriginal people was no longer spoken of lightly. Historians were uncovering the brutal realities of race war on the frontier. People like my mother – thoughtful and open-minded – were starting to think beyond the old heroic-pioneer stories. The turning point for Mum was a trip to Uluru in 1963, when for the first time she met Aboriginal people living on their traditional Country and speaking their own languages. That experience brought her face-to-face with the thing we know but don't know how to think about: that this was – and in important ways still is – an Aboriginal and Torres Strait Islander country with its own ways of living and its own languages and cosmologies. She saw that there might be things to be proud of in our past, but there was a lot to be ashamed of too.

That's why you can hear her distancing herself from what her mother told her. Granny Davis called Aboriginal people *blacks*, and my mother knew that was dismissive, even insulting. She's putting a layer of her own understanding between the story she heard and the one she tells: *the blacks, as they called them then.*

There was never a good word for the blacks. That's Mum's voice, too. I have a feeling she heard those actual not-good *words* – her mother mightn't have had any qualms about using them – but Mum wasn't going to repeat them. She's also obscuring the source of the words. Look – it's slid into the passive voice: *There was never a good word.* No one's actually uttering the not-good words.

Two things have happened in that slithery quick-step of grammatical footwork. It means that it's not necessarily Granny Davis who *never had a good word for the blacks* – it's the impersonal abstraction that the passive voice creates. It also means that, if by chance Granny Davis *was* one of the people who *never had a good word for the blacks*, it wasn't because she was an especially bad person. It was everyone. Mum's version of the story carries the comforting rationalisation: whatever happened, our lot was no worse than the others.

And what, exactly, did happen?

Well, as far as this account goes, nothing. This isn't about people anymore. It's about stories. *There were a lot of stories about women going out.* And Granny Davis hasn't just disappeared, she's become a negative – *No woman would ever be left in the house without a gun.* And who did the *leaving* of the gun? No one, it seems. The leaving of the gun has become a state, not an action. It would start to have the impact of the real if it was, *Her husband always made sure she had a gun when she was left alone in the house*. The events have been spread so thinly across the story that no one's responsible.

The nub of the story, and the heart of its silence, is where Mum says, *and – I don't know if they actually shot any of them.* That *and* – with a hesitation after it – that's a thought interrupted. Maybe she did know. If she knew, she'd have been ashamed, too ashamed to put the thought into words.

But she's not prepared to actually deny it. She could have said, *They didn't actually shoot any of them*, or even, *I don't think they actually shot any of them*. She fudged it, but she didn't falsify.

And – did they actually shoot *any of them*? I've read that at times the showing of the gun was enough. That might have been the case here, and of course I hope so. But the historical record is thin at that place and that time, so it may well be that I'll never know.

Say I did know, for sure, that the Davis gun was used against Aboriginal people. What would I feel? I'd be horrified and disgusted and ashamed – but no more horrified and disgusted and ashamed than I am already, knowing that others – strangers to me, not family – did so. The terrible thing about our past is the use of the guns (and other kinds of violence) against First Nations people. Who exactly owned the finger that pulled the trigger at any particular moment isn't really the point. The point is that all of us non-Indigenous Australians are the beneficiaries of that violence. In a way, even wondering what Sarah Davis did with the gun – did she shoot or didn't she? – is a kind of willed myopia, a resistance to looking at the bigger picture.

Now that I'm finally prepared to hear the family story, is it *guilt* that I feel? No, it's nothing as simple as that. For a start, you can only feel guilt for something you yourself did. But more than that, *guilt* suggests an equation: *guilt* on one side and *innocence* on the other. *Guilt* is something you can put right or balance out. You can apologise, give compensation, accept punishment. But the thing about this feeling is that there's no way to balance it with apology or compensation or punishment. They're important and necessary, but they don't erase it. What I'm left with is something complicated, something there doesn't quite seem to be a word for: the thing that happens when you've benefitted from a great wrong, but you weren't the one who actually did it.

Guilt is appropriate for one part of our legacy, though. What we should feel guilt for may not be the stealing itself, but the fact that we keep on refusing to address what the stealing has done. We've resisted listening to First Nations people. We go on rejecting ideas that they tell us will offer a way forward. We might tell ourselves that we don't need to feel guilt for the past. But we have to accept that we're guilty for what we're doing – or failing to do – in the present.

Mum could have left this whole story out of what she told me and no one would ever have known. Many a family storyteller has taken that path. But she didn't. Like an honest historian, she included all her sources, even if she was troubled by what they said. Her way around the dilemma was to pass the story on faithfully, but to put another frame around it, the frame of her own perspective.

And here I am, putting another frame around it in my turn. I know much more than she did about what happened in huts on the frontier, so I'm much more uncomfortable repeating it. That's why I'm unpicking it so obsessively, word by word. I'm doing the same balancing-act that Mum did: trying to own the story at the same time as distancing myself from it. Owning it, because anything else is evading the truth of what happened on the frontier. Distancing myself, because it's painful and shameful.

Granny Davis was *renowned for her stories*, yet only one has been embedded deeply enough in family memory to have survived as an actual scrap of narrative – and it's about *the blacks*. What does that mean? Were many of her stories about them, and this was the only one that people went on telling? If that's the case, why? Was it the most dramatic? Or was it the *least* dramatic, the least troubling?

Among the many family stories Mum told me, this is the only one that even mentions Aboriginal people. And really, given what we now know about what went on, is that surprising? When you think about it, the remarkable thing isn't that there's *only* one story about *the blacks* in our family history. The remarkable thing is that there's *even* one.

And now the story turns a corner.

> But Granny Davis had a name for giving food out. There was the terrible depression and drought that lasted about four years, and whoever came to the door she'd give them something, however ill she could afford it. Among the old photos there may still be one of her.

There's that fuzzy thing again, right there in the passive construction of the idea. *Had a name.* Who gave her that name? Was it white people or Aboriginal people? Or did Granny Davis give herself that name? Was it true, or a little bit true, or not true at all? If it was true, who did she give the food to? To *the blacks*? To white people?

That coda doesn't give any of the detail that would make it convincing. Its job isn't to draw a picture, but to counter the nasty fact of the gun. That word *but* is the hinge. She had the gun. *But* she had a name for giving out food. The *but* joins them together, and it keeps them apart. The picture of the woman in the house with the gun is covered straight away by this other thing. She did bad, but look, she did good as well.

Yes, well. She had the gun, so she could afford to be generous.

It's taken me a while to sort out the business of the name *Piallaway*. Apparently the word means "big talk" or "big meeting place" in the Gomeroi language. In the past the name seems to have referred to a big general area north-west of Currabubula. The area takes in several plains separated by ridges or clusters of hills, and several small watercourses.

Confusingly, one of the new people also used the word Piallaway to refer to a specific run within that big area, and another called his run Pialaway, with different spelling. When John Martin Davis's obituary said that he *died on his run, Piallaway*, it might mean that his property was called Piallaway, or that it was somewhere within that larger area. These days, Piallaway is the name of a property in the middle of the general Piallaway area.

In the trial, Davis said his station was *between the arms of the range, to the end of Spring Creek*. On the map I can see where he must have meant. It's a massive wedge of land between two arms of what is now called the Melville Range, with Spring Creek running straight down the middle of the wedge and joining Currabubula Creek.

It's ten minutes' drive from Currabubula, out along the Piallaway road. Then I turn onto a smaller road called Clowes Road that runs up the middle of the wedge. I think, Shouldn't it be called Davis Road? It occurs to me that if you wrote the word *Davis* by hand and not very clearly, someone could read it as *Clowes*. It's a moment's meaningless speculation. There was probably a Mr Clowes along here after there was a Mr Davis. But it reminds me again how easy it is for things to get misrecorded, misunderstood, misremembered. For the truth of things to be lost.

Clowes Road travels along next to Spring Creek. Where the road bends close to the watercourse you can see the furrow where water runs after rain. Today the furrow is a line of dusty rounded stones. Now and then there's the gleam of a pool of water, nothing bigger than a backyard fishpond. What a precious thing water is in this landscape. How easily used up. This is a landscape where the person who controls the water controls everything. In this corner of the country, I can see that Davis controlled it all.

There are paddocks cleared and ploughed for a crop, and there are clear grassy areas with sheep. I glimpse farmhouses, each one off behind a cattle grid and a big gate. Always a sign on the gate. *No Entry. No Trespassing. Private Property*. So how, exactly, did that wide-open land *with no stations marked* become a landscape where a fence runs tight beside the road on both sides and every single gate warns you off?

For the first time in my life, I'm curious about the nuts and bolts of how all those vast acres were transferred from the First

Nations to men like my great-great-grandfather. And I'm also thinking how sad and terrible it is that I've never wondered before. I've read books about frontier history but when it came to the land laws they seemed very complicated. Did I need to know all that detail? The big picture was clear enough: my lot just took it.

Now I see that sliding over the surface is one more evasion. The taking of the land is the heart of our history. Thinking that I didn't need to know exactly how it happened was just another way of not facing that history.

Turns out it was a boiling-frogs sort of thing. First there was the *squatting*. Davis would have heard about the good land beyond the limits of location. *Explorers* like Mitchell had reported on it, but in any case men with flocks and herds had already begun to push into that land. Davis and McCarthy would have set off from Davis's place in the Hunter Valley with a flock of sheep and kept going north till they found a stretch of land that didn't have anyone else's stock on it. They'd have got a hut up, maybe some stockyards, and sent the sheep out as a kind of walking version of all those *Private Property* signs.

Vast tracts had been taken over by squatters by the time the authorities – that is, the Colonial Office in London – realised they were losing control of the land beyond the limits of location. The first step was to formalise the situation by issuing depasturing licences. These simply gave the squatters permission to do what they'd already been doing, but by issuing the licences and charging a fee, the authorities established that they were in charge.

The next step, ten years later, was to establish a system of pastoral leases over those *runs* or *stations*. A lease suited both the squatters and the authorities. For the squatters, a lease gave security of tenure and a legal right to be there. For the authorities, it ensured that they retained control – the land was still owned by the Crown, and a lease could always be revoked. A lease also made sure that the squatters couldn't in the future claim freehold rights over the land on the basis of long occupation.

All you had to do to get this mighty windfall was apply. I haven't found Davis's application, but this is how his neighbour to the south, George Curtis, described his own boundaries:

> Curtis George.
> Name of Run – Pialaway.
> Estimated Area – 24 square miles.
> Estimated Grazing Capabilities – 5,000 Sheep.
>
> Bounded on the south by the bald ridges by the lower cattle camp to the westward, by the fall of the water from the Urarie Creek station to the south-east over a ridge which divides the Urarie Creek station to Carabubla, and by the northward by the Duri range, and the fall of the water to Pialaway, and by a marked tree line dividing McDougall's run from the Pialaway station.

The form itself did half the work of making theft seem legitimate. It bypassed the awkward realities of the original land grab by assuming that a piece of unmarked land was something of which you could ask, *Name of Run? Estimated Area?* – just as you might ask of a piece of surveyed freehold land.

Only the description of the boundaries gave the game away. There was no hiding the fact that the idea of the *run* having anything as definite as a *boundary* was a bit of wishful thinking. If you were to try to match up any of those descriptions with an actual piece of country, it would be tricky. *The bald ridges by the lower cattle camp to the westward* ... that could be almost anywhere.

But exactly where they were didn't matter. George Curtis could put any approximate thing down on the form, because this wasn't about actually *locating* a place. It was a piece of theatre: the performance of precision, underpinning the performance of legality.

By the time I'd read half-a-dozen descriptions like this, I was hating them. They were a declaration of possession imposed on the intimate body of the country itself, its private crevices of creeks and hills and the way the waters ran, those details taken down and used for the purposes of claiming ownership. It was ridiculous, of course, but I began to feel that the descriptions were a violation, as if the place were being forced to betray itself.

George Curtis had 24 square miles and Davis's other neighbour McDougall had 25 square miles. Davis's run was probably around the same size. If I were to walk around the perimeter of 25 square miles, I'd be walking 20 miles (around 30 ks). At an average walking speed of three miles an hour, it would take me most of a day to walk around Davis's run – that's if the ground was clear and flat, which of course it wasn't. That's a lot of land.

The pastoral leases were written by the authorities in London, and contained various conditions that ensured the land was not just claimed but also used. Those conditions were easily met. But there was one condition on every pastoral lease that was of huge significance – in fact it should have changed the whole shape and style of our history. It was a clause that acknowledged the prior claim of the First Nations, and it was designed in the hope that it might give them some degree of protection. The clause *reserve[d] to the Aboriginal Inhabitants of Our said Colony such free access to the said Run or parcel of Land hereby demised, or any part thereof, and to the trees and water thereon, as will enable them to procure the animals, birds, fish, and other foods on which they subsist.* The clause made it clear that Aboriginal people were not to be treated as trespassers. The land was to be used by both sets of people.

It was a well-meaning condition, but it was devised by men who didn't know how things worked on the ground on the other side of the world. The model informing their thinking was the nomad model. But the way Aboriginal people were physically managing the land was something closer to the farming-and-pastoral model, and the clause didn't address the requirements of that model.

The misconception about coexistence started with the fact that the animals Aboriginal people depended on were grass-eaters and were therefore in direct competition with the animals the strangers brought. The squatters worked at reducing that competition by killing as many kangaroos and emus as they could, leaving fewer for the hunters.

As well, the strangers wouldn't have understood the constant small-scale burning that kept the lures-and-traps system working. They'd see people walking out with firesticks, the grass flaming up, the fire spreading and burning their precious grass. They'd rush out on their horses, try to stop the burning, run the people off. Not understanding what they were seeing, they'd think it was deliberate troublemaking. It would give them a reason to do things they might have called *teaching the blacks a lesson.*

Would the Aboriginal people have tried to explain the sequence of carefully timed activities to the white people? Probably, but there was a language barrier, and the white people wouldn't have tried too hard to understand. They wouldn't want to know how wrong they were about the *nomad* thing, and it suited them to believe that *savages* could never have devised something so complicated and subtle. Over time the disruption blurred the carefully maintained hunting patterns and made them less effective.

The plant food, the daily staples, suffered from the coming of the new animals too. They grazed the plants more destructively than the native animals did. What grazing didn't kill, thousands of hard hooves did. Not to mention all the dung and urine on plants that die if they get too much nitrogen.

Then there's the water. Imagine John Martin Davis's sheep – he'd have had thousands, like George Curtis – coming to drink at those fishpond-sized pools along Spring Creek. By the time they'd drunk their fill there'd be nothing left but trampled mud.

Greater than any of those physical or material considerations, though, was the spiritual dimension, the cosmology embedded in the landscape. Unrecognised by the foreigners, but more significant than any fence or boundary marker, was the fact that each part of the land was the Country of a particular group, maintained through knowledge that was sacred and often secret. The profound relationship First Nations people had with the land was sustained through ceremonies and other acts of a spiritual nature. It needed much more than just *access*.

However, the real problem with the well-meaning condition on the lease was simpler than any of those factors. The fundamental problem was that it was ignored. The squatters ignored it, but so did the authorities. No one ever enforced it. Squatters assumed that having a lease gave them the right to control everything that happened on their land. They thought it gave them the right to treat Aboriginal people as trespassers, and that it was okay to keep them off by any means, up to and including shooting them dead.

Until 1996, no one seemed even aware of the existence of that clause. Only at that late stage was it pulled out of the oubliette it had been in for so long. It was then used as the basis of the legal argument in the *Wik* case. The argument was about whether those pastoral leases extinguished native title – in other words, whether the First Nations still had any rights over their traditional lands and waters. The court found that they did. Because of that long-forgotten clause, native title continued over leased land, coexisting with the rights of the leaseholder.

If the squatters had taken notice of that clause, or if any of the authorities who'd been issuing those leases for 150 years had enforced it, our history would be very different. The squatters would have been obliged to negotiate with the First Nations from the beginning, working out how to share the land. That's finally happening now, in some contexts, but it's 150 years too late for all those who were hounded off their land or killed.

Of course the Gomeroi pushed back. Like the Dharug, like the Darkinjung, like the Wonnarua, and every other group across the country, they used whatever means they could to defend their land.

They killed sheep and cattle, speared settlers, burned down huts, burned crops, took food, tools and clothes. Their guerilla strategies suited the situation and were hard to combat. They knew the landscape and could retreat to remote or hard-to-access places when the white men came after them. At first, they outnumbered the white men. Slow-to-load old guns were no match for the speed and silence of spears, and fire was a weapon the new people couldn't fight. Eventually, though, the equation tipped the other way: there were too many settlers, with better guns and plenty of horses, and diseases Aboriginal people had no defences against. But in the 1840s they pushed back so effectively in the Liverpool Plains that many colonists abandoned their runs.

Not Davis, though. It sounds as if he tried the king plate, he tried the gun. Maybe the other way round. Then he retreated to the relative safety of the main road and started the pub. But he kept the big spread of acres, kept it stocked with sheep and cattle and a stockman and shepherds. He worked it out somehow. Or maybe, like the man who held the lease to Myall Creek Station, the site of that well-recorded massacre, he left the *working-out* to his employees.

Did he ever happen to read that clause in his lease, and obey it? If he did, he'd have been one in a thousand.

I doubt if even the best researcher would know for sure where Davis's first hut was. But as I drive slowly up Clowes Road I'm auditioning likely spots. Maybe through there – can I make out a place where the grass is different, where a hut might have been? Or further over, where the trees seem to stand in a circle? Or what about here, where I can see the glitter of a few pools? Above them there's a comfortable rise where you'd be safe from floods. There's a side-track with a wide white gate across it and I can see a house further along, nearly hidden among trees. It's an obvious place to settle yourself in this landscape, and I pull in to the track and imagine the hut there, overlooking lovely undulating country with those big sprawling trees here and there, the ground between them covered with sheep-cropped grass.

I picture John Martin Davis arriving in the afternoon, in this golden light, horse and man casting a long shadow. Did he marvel at nature's beauty and nature's bounty? Was he maybe religious? Did he get down off his horse and on bended knees give thanks to God? Or was he calculating how many sheep to the acre this country could carry, and how much of it he could claim before he ran into the claim of some other man?

So let's imagine the hut up there among the trees, somewhere near where that house is. Imagine an afternoon like this one, the crickets making their sun-going-down song. If you look back towards the east, it's that lovely open grassland where the sun is still lighting up the golden distance. But in every other direction there's a feeling of shadows. The high steep ridges on either side of the valley are pressing in, thickly timbered slopes behind which, I know from the map, are more thickly timbered slopes.

There's the hut, and Sarah is in there. She's alone with the children because Davis is out on the run, miles away on his horse, checking on his shepherds and his flocks. Being alone in the hut wouldn't have felt peaceful, the way I'm feeling the place today. She might have felt vulnerable. The trees and bushes would make it easy to creep up on a person in a hut. As the sun went down she'd be listening – trying not to listen – for the crack of a twig under a bare foot. There'd be nowhere to run to: the open grasslands on one side, the steep rocky hillsides on the other. And in any case, there'd be no one, no neighbour, for miles and miles.

No wonder they got the pub going, quick as they could.

I *really* want to climb over the fence to walk over the land, under those venerable old trees, on that golden grass. I want to get close to it, connect with it. Feel the spirit of the place. Feel the land of my fathers – stolen though it was – under my feet.

There's a fence, of course, but I'm eyeing it for the weak point where it might be loose enough for me to slip through. I'm taking the first step towards it when a four-wheel drive appears behind me out of nowhere. It slows, stops. The dust it's made rolls forward over me. The engine throbs. Someone winds down their window and a big bearded face looks out at me.

You right, love?

The tone is more or less neutral. So is the face in the window. I'm probably on his land. His front drive. His white gate. He's seen me heading to the fence, will have seen I was planning to slip through it.

I'm an old woman, so he's curious rather than suspicious. He's ready to help if need be. Still, he wants to know what I'm up to, because it's his place.

No, no worries, I'm fine! I call back. I gesture vaguely with my phone and head towards my car.

Okay, love, he says, and keeps going up the track. I take a photo or two of the view, just for appearances, and out of the corner of my eye I see him get out to open the gate. He uses the action to glance back at me. More than glance. He's watching. I make another vague wave and he does a stiff wave back. He watches while I get back in the car.

I do a five- or six-point turn, I don't want to get stuck or hit his fence. He's still watching as I finally get around. I put on my indicator like an idiot, as if the place where his front drive meets the track is a busy intersection. I'm in a fluster, can feel the blood hot in my cheeks.

So much for wanting to feel the land of my fathers under my feet! I'm laughing at myself so much that the car skitters for a moment on the gravel as I turn and accelerate away.

Further up in the end of the wedge it's more heavily wooded and there are no more farmhouses, no more sheep. Just majestic old-man trees with thick trunks and enormous spreading crowns, standing up to their knees in long pale grass.

After a time the road fades, bends down towards the creek, and simply ends. The high ridges rise all around me, wild country of bush and rocks. I pull over and get out, the quiet pouring in like smooth liquid as I stand on the dust of the road. The afternoon sun slants softly, filling the grass with a cloud of radiance. There's a world of sound here. There's the whispering of the trees, the quick twittering of birds, the long, sad cry of a crow, and that almost-too-high-pitched-to-hear insect thrum that you get in the bush once you're not crashing through it. When you stop going somewhere, what you hear is the life of the place, going about its business whether or not human beings are there to notice it.

I'm looking up at the hillside of trees, a crowd of all ages and different kinds. Each one fell as a seed and put its roots down, growing bravely in the dry stony soil of the slope, each one living its life in the midst of all its brothers and sisters, all growing beside each other so thick and stubborn. The place is dynamic, it's an organism, it's alive – even the rocks and dirt are part of the knitted-together life of the place. Standing in the heart of this folded land is like being within a vast living creature, its existence progressing at a slow scale that makes human life a flicker of nothing.

I realise I've got that thickening in my throat that you feel when you're getting ready to cry. What is happening, what's this sadness welling up in me, this vast sorrow?

Perhaps I don't need to know. Or perhaps it's obvious. Perhaps it's the only proper way to feel when you're standing on the soft dust of this country, in this place of trees and the whispering of leaves stroking over each other, a place of such piercing beauty where so many ugly things happened.

THE MYALL WATERHOLES

A hundred and seventy-five years ago two men went head-to-head in court. Andrew McDougall claimed that John Eales had trespassed on his land at Piallaway by allowing his sheep and cattle to depasture there. The case went on for three days. Twenty-five witnesses were called, including McDougall's neighbour John Martin Davis. Depasturing licences were produced. Maps were sketched and then re-sketched by others with the landmarks in different places. At the end of the three days, the judge summed up for the jury. The dispute was about the matter of trespass, he said. That went to the matter of who owned the land in dispute. That, in turn, went to how ownership might be established. In the case of the land under dispute, ownership was essentially a matter of *long and continuous occupation*.

Guided by those considerations, the jury found for the plaintiff. Long and continuous occupation of a tract of land made Andrew

McDougall its owner. John Eales had trespassed on his property. He was to pay 350 pounds.

Of course, Andrew McDougall had no more right to the place than John Eales. They were both trespassers on land that belonged to other people by right of long and continuous occupation. Those people were never explicitly mentioned in the trial, but they were there in the room, because nearly every witness referred to a feature of the landscape they called the *Myall Waterholes*. As far as those men were concerned, the Myall Waterholes were nothing more than a convenient landmark they used to make their case about who owned what. McDougall had tried for a while to call them the McDougall Waterholes, but that name had never stuck. Those landmarks were still being called the Myall Waterholes at the trial, nearly thirty years after the white men first came and saw *the land all open before them*. To my ears, the persistence of that name in so many mouths, over so many years, was an unintended but undeniable acknowledgement of those other *long and continuous* owners. This was Aboriginal land, and at some smothered level of awareness all those men knew that.

The word *myall* was first written down in 1818. It was a colonist's transcription of a word from the language of the people who lived around Sydney, and he thought it meant *stranger* or *ignorant person*. The person who said the word and tried to explain its meaning may have been talking about another group of Aboriginal people. But he or she might have been talking about the colonists. They were strangers, after all, and they were certainly ignorant about the place they'd come to.

But the colonists began to use the word to refer to the people they were displacing, as if *they* were the ignorant strangers. Specifically, the word was used to refer to the *wild blacks,* as opposed to the *blacks* who were interacting with the colonists, the kind who might have been given a king plate. *Wild blacks* were the ones who might spear you. They were dangerous and frightening, and the word the colonists used for them came to signal contempt and denigration.

The word persists in many placenames. There's the infamous Myall Creek, but there are also the Myall Lakes, the Myall River, Myall Park, the Myall Ranges, Myall Springs and others. Those names acknowledge – in a backhanded way – a truth that the colonists usually ignored or denied: the place belonged to the First Nations.

Then there are the Myall Waterholes at Piallaway. Different witnesses placed them in different relation to other natural features, but everyone used them as the most significant landmark. You can see why. This is dry country. Until you get to Werris Creek, a fair way to the west, there are no permanent watercourses. All those witnesses had a clear mental image of the Myall Waterholes because without them, their sheep and cattle would have perished.

What I'm finding interesting about the Myall Waterholes is that they seem to have disappeared. Possibly not out of the landscape, but certainly off the map. I've looked on my 1:25,000 topographic map of Piallaway, and there are various little blue specks here and there, but they're all unnamed, and none are in a cluster as the word *waterholes* suggests. Like so much else about the past, they've disappeared.

This afternoon, after another night in Tamworth, I'm back on the bitumen of Piallaway Road, poring over the map, because I've made up my mind to try to find them. Standing in that gorgeous place up there at the end of Clowes Road yesterday seems to have shifted something. Just for the moment I've had enough, more than enough, of thinking about John Martin Davis. I have some obscure feeling of honouring the Gomeroi people in this area by finding the waterholes named for them, as if that might provide an entry into another zone, or make a kind of time machine, to repopulate this place with the people who were here long before Davis and McDougall and Eales.

I pore over my map, trying to find any of the places mentioned in the trial, but for a person wanting a time machine, these days there's only big geology, the unalterable shape of mountains and plains. The map, with its faint contour lines showing how the land goes up and down, makes it clear that Piallaway is essentially a huge flat expanse, with a mass at one side that bears the unromantic name of Piallaway Paddock Mountain. I'm thinking that water must flow down from that mountain when it rains, so the Myall Waterholes might be somewhere around its base. I decide to drive around it as closely as the roads will let me.

I start with one that runs more or less around the south side of the mountain. I see a cluster of bare ridges that could be the *bald ridges* George Curtis mentioned. I see some pointy, sharp-looking rocks standing upright on the top of another hill and wonder if they're the Piallaway Needles marked on my map. But there's nothing on this land that looks even damp, let alone anything that could be called *waterholes*.

And now the side road that my map shows as continuing around the south of the mountain turns out to be the driveway up to someone's distant house. There's a big gate. *No trespassers*. I turn around and speed along back to the road that will take me around to the north. I'm conscious of the enormous plume of yellow dust behind me. I picture the people up there on their verandah, hearing the car and seeing the dust. They'd know all their neighbours' cars and the noises they make. Even before I'm in view, they'd know I'm a stranger.

The day is becoming an endless time of glaring sun, dry paddocks, long stretches of level yellow road. And speed. I'm going too fast for this gravelly road, barrelling along with a kind of anxiety, as if the Myall Waterholes will run away if I don't hurry. It seems that the more I'm not finding them, the more doggedly determined I am, and I don't know why. Is it nothing more than the tourist urge, that compulsion to see the Eiffel Tower for yourself, no matter how many pictures of it you've seen?

On the map it looks as though the road branches off to continue around the mountain, but when I get to where that road should be there's only another private track with a gate – *Private Property* – and a big silo off in the distance. The road heads out into flat land, as flat as the top of a table, with some kind of low dark crop growing on it. My map tells me – I think – that I'm heading out onto the Breeza Plain. I drive on in the hope that there'll be another road that will take me where I want to go.

I seem to be driving for a long time on a very straight dirt road across this plain and I'm definitely heading in the wrong direction. The road shows no sign of being about to loop back towards the mass of mountain, now shrinking in the rear-view mirror. And no waterholes. How can something so significant disappear – not just off the face of the map, but off the face of the land?

My anxiety has taken on a more specific flavour. There's something about the flatness, the uniformity of the dark crop, the sun beating down. Suddenly I'm spooked. I need a stop, a reset, a think.

And I need to give up on finding the Myall Waterholes. They were here, and they probably still are, somewhere. They – like this whole landscape – were part of the home and heartland of the Gomeroi people, and I'm indignant that their name has vanished. But in the big picture of all the erasures, that particular vanishing isn't even a blip. Looked at that way, my narrow determination to find them feels self-centred, even arrogant. I want to put myself into the picture with them, but is that any more meaningful than the way tourists want to have their photo taken with the Eiffel Tower? It's a way of owning a piece of something, of inserting yourself into its story, when really, it's not yours.

Turning around is a bit of a business. The road's very narrow and there's a deep ditch on each side. I inch backwards and forwards, backwards and forwards, and finally I'm facing the other way, towards the massy hill. I go carefully and slowly, until at last I'm at the *Private Property* gate and the silo, and past it – at last – there's a clump of trees and, miracle of miracles in this tightly fenced country, a place to pull off the road under a group of trees.

The shade is a relief after that bald plain with its industrial-scale whatever-it-was. In fact, it's altogether a very sweet corner, with the enormous old trees clustered around me. Leaves are rustling and a bird's tweeting insistently. When the bird stops it's very quiet. I imagine everything watching the interloper – the birds, the lizards, the snakes, all the small life of the place.

Over the fence there are five or six brown cows, arranged picturesquely under the trees, a Constable painting in the middle of Piallaway. And there's a rather winsome calf rubbing its head on a leaning tree. They could be distant descendants of McDougall's cattle, I suppose. The calf stares at me in a short-sighted way.

Lifts its feet. It's got socks on every leg from the mud it's standing in, a wide brown puddle.

Now I notice that the wires of the fence between me and the cows are hung with muddy grass and leaves. That's why there's a puddle – it's from a recent flood. I look behind me and see that more stuff's caught on that fence too. I'm standing in a long shallow indentation in the land that must be a seasonal watercourse. There'd be a whole string of puddles ahead of me and behind me. Some of them might even be big enough to call a waterhole.

I spread the map out on the bonnet. There's the Breeza Plain where I've just been, and there's the place with the silo. If I'm where I think I am, I'm not far from two of the unnamed blue specks, a pair of little banana shapes in a line. I can't see them, and I'm not going to get through the fence to look for them, but the puddles more or less line up with them. I'm prepared to believe they're the Myall Waterholes.

I'm as excited as if I've just unearthed buried treasure. I get out my pen, ridiculously pleased, and carefully draw a line of circles on the map to represent the puddles. I do a neat arrow to the banana shapes and write *Myall Waterholes.* There! No – that looks too sure of itself. I come back in with the pen and add a question mark.

Question mark and all, I feel something's been done, although I'm wondering now why it seemed so important. What was all that frantic rushing about to find them? What's been prodding me on for these last few hours, everything else forgotten? If they'd been marked on the map, I probably wouldn't have given them a second thought. It's the very fact that they're not marked that made me so determined to find them. They were marked on the map of everyone's minds, back in those long-ago days. They were the one ghost of an acknowledgement of who was here. Then they were erased. I suppose what I wanted so much to do was to un-erase them. To do what I've just done with such satisfaction: put them back on the map.

Well, the white map. Wherever the Myall Waterholes really are, and whatever they were called before the colonists came, they don't need me to find them. They've always been on their own map.

GOONOO GOONOO

After another night in a cabin in the caravan park at Tamworth, I'm ready for the next generation. John Martin Davis and Sarah Davis had nine children. The fourth was called Sarah Catherine, as her mother was, so for a while there were two Sarah Catherine Davises. Then in 1867 the younger Sarah Catherine, my great-grandmother, married Thomas Maunder and became Sarah Maunder.

For most of my life, how everyone fitted together was a vague muddle in my mind. The day at Wisemans Ferry might have been the first time Mum told me the family stories, but it wasn't the last. She'd been given the stories to pass along, and that was a responsibility she wasn't going to shirk. I don't think she recounted them to my brothers – she had a sense that the family stories were an heirloom handed down through the women. What she couldn't understand was why I didn't seem to want to accept that gift. When she started in again about Solomon Wiseman or John Martin Davis I didn't even pretend to be interested.

Why? I'm trying now, a lifetime later, to remember what I felt when she launched into the well-worn anecdotes. It was something almost like embarrassment. To my ears there was a whiff of *look how special we are* about them. It wasn't that the people were wealthy or famous – it wasn't that kind of simple snobbery – but it was that we had these stories. We had that connection to the place. That was a kind of wealth, and not everyone had it.

Even later, when I used some of the stories as a way into some of my novels, I found it hard to sort out the generations and I didn't want to look too hard. I was happy for the characters in the books to be – as I often said, when talking about them – *representative* of their time and place, rather than specifically my forebears. Outside the fiction I wrote based on them, their actuality was something I didn't want to engage with deeply.

But being on Piallaway has somehow burned off that comfortable vagueness. Vagueness? Let's call it by its real name: refusal. Getting mixed up about which generation was which, thinking it was all too complicated and boring, was another version of looking away. Now I'm ready to take on the details of the legacy I've inherited, to know exactly how I'm connected to the things that happened on this country. It's not that complicated after all.

And it's not that far away. Sarah Catherine Maunder died in 1918, but her husband, Thomas Maunder, didn't die till 1931. That's only ten years before the elder of my two brothers was born. Very nearly within living memory. That's how close all this history is. No wonder it's easier to look away.

This morning I'm driving to a place that was once a vast sheep run called Goonoo Goonoo, a few ks east of Currabubula. It wasn't taken up by a squatter, but given as a grant to a company with shareholders in Britain and Australia. I'm going there because Goonoo Goonoo gets a walk-on part in the family story about Thomas Maunder. This is how my mother tells it:

> Thomas Maunder was a Cockney (born within the sound of Bow bells, he was proud to say) and migrated to Australia as an indentured labourer when he was seventeen, in about 1860. I don't know how many of his family came with him, but there was certainly one sister and they both went to work on arrival on Goonoo Goonoo Station.
>
> This was one of the biggest stations in the north. It stretched from Quirindi to Tamworth and was managed by the King family – he was one of the early governors and these were his descendants.
>
> Mum over and over again told the story of the early King who was running Goonoo Goonoo when her father arrived – Grandfather's sister died on the station and this awful man made him (Grandfather) dig her grave! Quite apart from the hard work, which Grandfather wasn't used to, it was a cruel thing to make a brother do.
>
> Another story about that same King – when he had to speak to any of his underling workers, boundary riders and stockmen, he used to keep his distance, and if they dared

> approach him he would say, "Stand back, my man, stand back, at least 10 yards, you harbour the flies so!" Another dreadful thing he had to do, according to Mum: he had to take three rams – rams are notoriously difficult to deal with – from one end of the station to the other – a huge distance, from Tamworth to Quirindi. He had to do this on his own and without a dog, and he an inexperienced London Cockney.

When I heard the story about the rams as a child I wasn't impressed. I had a sentimental image – from my childhood reading of *Heidi*, I suppose – of docile fluffy sheep being shepherded by a sweet young girl. The smock. The quaint shepherd's crook. When Mum told me about Thomas Maunder taking those rams from Tamworth to Quirindi I thought, How hard could it be?

Since my days of reading *Heidi* I've had a bit of experience with sheep. Trying to make them go where you want is harder than you'd think. They'll baulk, turn, leap, swivel, rush left, rush right, push past you in a panic. Somewhere in the sheeps' DNA is a memory of escaping a mountain lion, and they think the feeble human flapping its hat is that mountain lion.

I've decided to make the same journey that young Thomas Maunder did with those rams. Not walking, the way he did, and not with sheep. I'll drive on the nice smooth New England Highway. These days Goonoo Goonoo is much shrunken from its heyday, but I'm starting where its northern boundary used to be, at Tamworth. Quirindi, the southern end, is around 70 ks south. Indeed, a *huge distance* for a person on foot.

As I leave Tamworth the land opens out into a golden-grassed, gently undulating plain. Here and there are patches of bush but mostly it's open country with big old trees scattered at more or less regular intervals. It's the *gentleman's park* thing again. Everything is very crisp and hard-edged in the clean early-morning air. Far off to the east there's a blue range of sharp mountains. They look like a painted stage set, a city person's idea of what distant mountains look like.

I'm trying to imagine it back in 1832 when Edward Parry picked it for the Australian Agricultural Company. When he first saw it there'd have been great mobs of roos and emus. There'd have been the fires and huts of Gomeroi people somewhere around here, and families working the land in the ways they knew. Now it's cattle up to their bellies in sweet grass.

The original homestead of Goonoo Goonoo is 20 ks south of Tamworth. As I whiz past I glimpse the homestead and outbuildings on a soft east-facing slope. There are big comfortable trees and a sense of the buildings nestling into the land. These days the old buildings have been made into a posh place to stay. I could have spent the night there, where my great-grandfather had to *stand back, my man, you harbour the flies so!* The thought didn't appeal. I'm a bit sickened by the idea of those old buildings, the site of so much toil and human misery in the past, being dolled up.

In the west – on my right – a long high ragged ridge, steep and stony and covered with thin trees and bushes, has approached and now runs along parallel with the highway. Looking at the map I can see that it's the other side of the same range that was beside me all the way up from Quirindi a couple of days ago. Quirindi and Currabubula and Piallaway are to the west of the range, Goonoo Goonoo is on the east of it. A sheer rock wall runs along the top like fierce bared teeth. It's a stern and powerful and forbidding piece of country. As I drive south it dominates the landscape.

You can see how the Gomeroi people in this area would have been squeezed. There were new people over the range at Currabubula and Piallaway, where I was yesterday. There were more of them here at Goonoo Goonoo. The steep arid ridge between those two sets of pushy strangers might have been one of the few places to retreat to for a time. But like the dry hills beside Mogo Creek, this ridge wouldn't have offered long-term refuge. By the time Thomas Maunder was here with his three rams in the 1860s, the guns had been speaking all over the Liverpool Plains for decades. To survive, Gomeroi people had had to adapt.

Their leverage should have been their moral and timeless claim to the land, but that cut no ice with the Australian Agricultural Company's shareholders. The only thing that worked in Aboriginal people's favour was that the graziers needed their labour. Some Gomeroi people made the choice to stay on their land and work for rations or – sometimes – cash. It was a pragmatic adaptation to the new reality. It wasn't good, but it meant that they weren't shot at, they didn't starve and they could stay on their Country.

The road runs parallel with the range, as the track Thomas Maunder followed would have done. Just keep the ridge on your right, they'd have told him. You can't go wrong. But of course you could, quite easily, because some 20 ks south of the homestead the road begins to bend and weave through a muddled confusion of hills and gullies. The sign calls this area Lindsay's Gap, but the place isn't as straightforward as the sign makes it sound. In every direction there's something that could be a *gap*. For a person wrangling three rams, with only a rough track marked by the occasional blazed tree, it would have been easy to choose the wrong opening in the ups-and-downs.

That poor boy. The forbidding ridge with its hard grey bones of rock, this tumbled place of confusing hillocks – it wouldn't have been like anything he'd ever seen before. How did he do it, a boy who'd been a baker's apprentice in London and who probably hadn't ever handled a sheep?

From Lindsay's so-called Gap, I see on the map that there are two ways to get to Quirindi. The first way, through Wallabadah, is longer but my map shows it as level land, an easy journey. The second runs along beside Jacob and Joseph Creek. The map shows the creek and the road weaving and dodging through the scumbled end of that mighty ridge. That way would be shorter, though probably harder going.

But on the map the road is a firm red line, not a dotted one, and what I can see from here looks fine. A few hills, nothing too imposing. The road – dirt, but wide and well-graded – winds between grassy paddocks, under big graceful trees. Sparkling Jacob and Joseph Creek flows swiftly over its stones, clear and cold, a stream out of a children's picture book. I don't know what Tom Maunder did, but I'm going to cut through the short way.

At first it's gorgeous. The yellow dust of the road bends accommodatingly along the face of the country, around spurs of hillside, down into a low place beside the creek, up the other side and around the next spur. Around me on each side are high ridges but the road follows the creek along the bottom of this tender green place, with stretches of pasture between stands of gums, a landscape on a human scale, every curve in the road revealing some inviting new corner.

I keep stopping and getting out and trying to photograph this beauty. Those grey boulders bursting through the grass. The gauzy effect of these delicate trees with their slender leaves hanging down. In a fold in the land, smoke haze softens the scene with blue mist and the sun gleams through it with a bronzed, dim quality.

I'm in a kind of trance of pleasure, pushing on bend after bend to see the next lovely vista. But dark clouds are gathering, and now they're blocking out the sun. Suddenly the postcard-ready road winding under the trees looks like what it is: isolated and rough. I realise there's no mobile reception here in the depths of these ridges. Am I really on the right road, will this ever get to Quirindi or did I take a wrong turn somewhere? Am I pressing on and on into nowhere? Suddenly that sweet landscape always offering another inviting bend becomes oppressive.

And the road has become something of an ordeal. It keeps crossing the creek, and every time it does I have to drive through a couple of inches of water. I'm not concerned that I might get swept away, but I am apprehensive – more and more with each causeway – of getting stuck. The first two were concreted, but as I press on further into this tumbled land the causeways are gravel and mud. I try to remember all the things I've been told about driving through creeks: get out and look for the best route, back up a bit so you can cross steadily – not too fast but not too slow.

Finally I go over one that's wider than any of the others, and deeper. Halfway across I feel the steering wheel loosen in my hands.

The wheels aren't quite doing that terrible spinning-helplessly thing that I've experienced a couple of times in my life – they're gripping, but only just. Calm, I tell myself. Take a breath. Whatever you do, don't stamp your foot on the accelerator, the way you're longing to. The brave little car grinds along, the wheels making a scary sloshing noise, but finally the steering wheel comes to life in my hands and I'm through.

But what about the next one? I picture what's going to happen: the wheels finally giving up, whining and spinning in the mud. Would I do best to set off walking and hope that a house would appear between the trees, and some cheerful family would greet me and produce a tractor to haul me out? Or should I sit tight in the car and wait for someone to come along? I haven't met a single vehicle all this time, and now I'm trying to remember how far back it was that I last saw a house. It seems a long way. I imagine a great dark night-time silence settling around me, the stars cold in a black sky.

I'm not frightened. Not really. I remind myself this isn't the outback where people get lost and die. I've got plenty of water and enough snacks in the car to keep me going. A blanket in the back. I could hunker down, through the night if I had to, till a car came along.

Then, thank goodness, the ridges on either side peel back, the road straightens, and I can see flat land up ahead. Now I have the luxury of thinking that the fear I felt was useful. I can look back indulgently and tell myself it was all good research. If Tom Maunder had chosen that shortcut, I think he'd have been frightened in that tangle of country, and now I have a hint of what he might have felt.

But the fear has peeled back a layer of skin. I know something now that I didn't know before, and it's not about Tom Maunder, it's about me. I'm a visitor here, and like all visitors, I'm looking at the place through the lens of pleasure. Am I enjoying being here? Is it pretty enough for a photo? But a landscape isn't a picture for my pleasure. It's a serious thing, a machine for living. People have had to work with it to meet the basic human needs: water, food, shelter, and this picturesque place has filled those needs for millennia. Every one of those pretty creekside nooks where I got out and took yet another photo of a lovely tree, lovely light, the play of sunlight on water – every one of those places was life itself for all the people who knew it as the physical manifestation of a profound cosmology. They were part of it in a different way from someone pointing a camera at it and whispering, *Oh, wow*.

I've heard many of my fellow non-Indigenous Australians say how connected they feel to our country, how much they love it. How deeply their roots go into it. How keenly they miss it when they're not on it. How important it is to their sense of who they are. I understand their feelings and share them. This is my home and my heartland. It's the only place I truly know, and my love for it is part of who I am. But I'm seeing that a love like mine can turn into something like fear as soon as the sun goes down and the road gets tricky.

When we talk about how we love our country, we're not wrong, but we might be missing something. Maybe *love* is something you apply to something outside yourself. If you'd lived in this beautiful place for untold generations – known it, shaped it, trusted it to supply everything you needed – what you'd feel for all its lovely corners would be something essential, something more like a dimension of your own being. The people of the First Nations knew their Country would hold them and provide for them and give spiritual shape to their lives, through darkness as well as sunlight, through rain and drought as well as a perfect sunny day. That's a different kind of love.

Now that I'm thinking about that other way of relating to a place, my own *love* – that overused word – for this pretty landscape doesn't feel adequate. A person could pity someone with such a limited way of feeling, the way Inuit people must pity us for not realising that there are seventeen kinds of snow.

I've told the story about the three rams to a few friends who know about sheep and the consensus was that it would be pretty much impossible. Put them on a cart, said one person. Tie them together, said another. They all agreed that three sheep would be much harder than ten sheep, because sheep want to be a herd, and three isn't enough to be a herd. Each one of those rams would have had its own confused idea about what it should be doing. If they'd got away from Maunder and run into that buckling of hills or that vast open grassland, he'd never have seen them again.

Being here on the ground, having come through that Jacob and Joseph experience, I'm hearing the story with new ears. To tell the truth, I'm thinking it's baloney. It's like the snake-swallowing-the-ball story – one more reinforcement of the heroic pioneer legend. I can imagine Thomas Maunder telling some version of it to his children. Three rams! All the way from one end of Goonoo Goonoo to the other! No dog! They're open-mouthed with admiration. Years later they tell it to their own open-mouthed kids.

But whether it's true, or partly true, or frankly made up, being here, looking back at the tumbled landscape I've just come through, tells me something else, something that happened in the silence behind the story. Whatever shape the event really took, I'm guessing that Tom Maunder felt *they* were watching him, and he might have been right. The *blacks,* as he'd have called them. He'd have heard stories from the old hands. They'd have told him what had happened to other shepherds, out there, alone with the sheep on someone else's place.

Even now, it's the thing about the country. It looks empty, but someone's always watching. You go for a walk, you don't see a soul, but later someone says, Oh, did you have a good walk? Friendly, but letting you know it's their place. Reminding you that you're just passing through.

The First People knew every inch of their Country. They knew who was on it, and whether or not they belonged there. By the time Tom Maunder came to Goonoo Goonoo, there had been thirty years of strangers walking onto Gomeroi land with sheep and cattle. But who knows, there could have been Gomeroi people up there on that ridge, watching Tom Maunder from the moment he left the stockyards up near the Peel, battling the rams all the way down the miles to Quirindi. I'm imagining them laughing at him. They might even have felt a bit sorry for him, floundering along, sweating and shouting and swearing, flapping away at the flies, glancing around at where he could feel the invisible people watching. There might have been – there could be still! – a story among them about a boy trying to make three rams go where he wanted them to go – someone making everyone laugh, mimicking the white boy all alone in a foreign landscape.

It's vivid in my imagination because it's the mirror image of the story my family tells. Same dirt, same sky, same trees. I'm seeing two stories happening on the same country, but only one of them has been part of the tales my family has told itself.

FOREST FARM

Tom Maunder timed his migration well, because a year after he arrived, the government took the next step in the long gradual business of stealing the country. It had given the squatters leases to their runs, but now they were going to take some of that land back and give it to other people. The idea was to break up the vast estates that made the squatters too powerful and independent, and give other people a chance to get some land.

The 1861 *Land Acts* allowed anyone who could pay the deposit to go onto any of those pastoral leases and *select* whatever bit he liked the look of, up to 320 acres. The government could do that because the squatters only had leases, not freehold titles. They were tenants, and in theory their land could have all been taken back by their landlord, the Crown, and redistributed. In a fantasy world of justice, it could even have been distributed back to its original owners.

But selection was different. Selectors *bought* the land they selected – paid the government a pound an acre for it, and got a title deed to the freehold. In legal parlance that bit of land became *alienated.* British law used the word to mean it was alienated from its previous existence as Crown land. But the word had a deeper accuracy: the land was indeed *alienated*, deeply and permanently, from the people whose land it had always been. The squatters had *opened up* the land, the way a burglar opens up a house. The selectors were then free to walk in – in fact, the government encouraged them to walk in – make a *selection*, and take legal possession of it. From then on, it was part of a chain of buying and selling. It would never again be anything other than private property.

Naturally, the holders of those pastoral leases made it as hard as they could for the selectors. They made selections themselves, and they also selected in the names of their children and their mothers-in-law and their aunts and uncles and cousins twice removed. Their own selections took the best parts of the run, or cut the rest off from sources of water, or marooned stretches of land without access. There was trickery and there was violence. Still, thousands and thousands of men like my great-grandfather managed to get land.

The image in my mind, as I take on board exactly how this massive *alienation* happened, is those pictures we see on the news: a city street full of burning cars, police in riot gear, and men running out of smashed-open shops cradling televisions in their arms with a look of astonished glee. *Look what I scored!*

> When Sarah Davis married Thomas Henry Maunder he was still a farm labourer. He must have had plenty of go in him, because he gathered enough money to get a little bit of land – selections in the first place. I presume it was the Davis family who helped him to get a property. It was called Forest Farm, not far from Currabubula, and as he was a hard worker he did well. He was a famous shearer in his day and held the record at one time for shearing the greatest number of sheep in a day – with the blades, very hard work. Later, when he had his own children, he made them stay home from school to shepherd the sheep and work hard in the paddocks and the house.

The *little bit of land* Tom Maunder *got* in about 1865 was right on the western edge of Goonoo Goonoo, where the plain runs up against the frowning mass of the ridge. I'm driving there now, on the narrow dirt road leading west from Goonoo Goonoo homestead towards Forest Farm, a distance of around 10 ks. It's more of that wide open landscape, with the looming mass of the ridge straight ahead. My eye is caught by two huge flocks of white cockatoos wheeling above the paddocks like schools of fish, showing their dark upper wings against the clouds, then disappearing as they heel and turn together, white birds vanishing against white cloud.

He'd have known the whole area from working on it as a shepherd, and he chose cannily. It wasn't the worst land – it had some water and it wasn't too far from the village of Currabubula, around the corner of the range. It wasn't the best, either – it was a *forest* farm, so it must have been fairly heavily timbered. From a grazing point of view that made it second- or third-rate land. But it might have been worth putting up with that to bypass any potential trouble with the Australian Agricultural Company.

The place that used to be Forest Farm now has a big gate with video surveillance. There's a farmhouse and sheds in among spreading European trees. There's no forest here now. As soon as he got the place, Maunder would have set about clearing it. He wanted to clear it for his sheep, of course, but it was also one of the conditions of selection. You had to actually live on the place (unlike the squatters, who often lived elsewhere), and you had to do *improvements.* If you didn't, you'd lose the land.

Improvements meant clearing the trees, putting up a house and yards, and replacing native grass with imported kinds. And fencing. When Maunder first lived here, a fence was still a luxury – wire was expensive and wooden fences were labour-intensive – but he'd have fenced the perimeter of his place as soon as he could. It wouldn't have taken all that long for those 320 acres to be cleared back to open paddocks where sheep grazed and crops grew, and to be populated by a household of foreign men, women, children, horses, dogs and sheep.

Private property like these selections, locked in by a title deed and the sacred bond of purchase, was another turn of the screw for the First Nations. Unlike the big pastoral leases such as Davis's, with vague, unmarked boundaries, the selectors' boundaries were unambiguous. Under British law, that meant anyone who came over a fence was a trespasser, and the person inside the fence was within his rights to keep them out. There was nothing on a selector's title deed – not even the hot air of that forgotten clause on the pastoral leases – that might stay a man's hand.

The selections were something new out here: small farms, worked as intensively as the climate allowed. They were modest, family-run enterprises. The stories Mum tells make it clear that Tom Maunder relied on his children as his unpaid labour force. The sons shepherded the sheep, helped with the harvest, worked alongside their father clearing and fencing. The daughters took their turn as shepherds too, as well as doing all the invisible but unremitting work in the house and the yard.

What that meant was less employment for Aboriginal people. The coming of small-scale farming made it more difficult for them to stay on Country and cobble together a living from a mix of station employment and traditional subsistence. They looked for ways to adapt to the changed circumstances. Some pushed for land to be given to them, and some succeeded, though the amounts of land were small. Eighty-five Aboriginal reserves were set up in New South Wales in the last decade of the nineteenth century, around half of them initiated by Aboriginal people. Other land was proclaimed as independent Aboriginal farms.

When they were first established, the reserves and farms might have seemed a way forward. On the reserves, people could come and go, working for wages or rations on settlers' farms, while continuing at least some traditional food gathering on their reserved land. On some reserves – for a while – it was even still possible to come together for a modified version of the important traditional ceremonies. On the independent farms, intimate knowledge of place and climate meant that the families who worked them were successful.

For Aboriginal people at that time, displaced from their Country, their choices were limited. The land they were given was often poor, unwanted by the whites, and it was a microscopic fraction of what had been taken from them. But it might have seemed that to have a piece of land *reserved* for you by the government, for your exclusive use, was the best option in a landscape of bad ones.

I've learned all this from recent reading and conversations. The fact that – at least early on – Aboriginal people initiated some of the reserves came as a surprise, and I'd never heard about those independent farms and how successful they were. Along with all the other convenient myths about Aboriginal people, one myth I'd absorbed was that they were victims. Not passive – I'd known for a long time how vigorously they defended their Country – but defeated. What I've recently learned is the many ways they adapted, often strategically and effectively, to the new situation, making use of whatever chinks of opportunity the white world left them and pressing for more when they could. I'd grown up with the idea of them as people locked into a static culture that was unable to adapt. That was just one more stereotype that reduced them to something smaller and weaker than they really were.

But the new people kept moving the goalposts, so every successful adaptation had to be adapted in its turn. The Aborigines Protection Board was established with the ostensible aim of advocating for Aboriginal people. But before long it was using its power to impose government efforts at social engineering on the people it was supposed to be protecting. It began to use the reserves as a way to implement the policy of segregation, and Aboriginal people were pressured to move to them. One especially cynical way was to exploit Aboriginal people's recognition of the power that came from having a white education. Schools in the towns were allowed to exclude Aboriginal children. The board could take advantage of that, setting up schools on reserves as a way of persuading people to move to them. The catch was that those schools weren't as good as the schools for white children and they only went up to Grade Three.

Part of the justification for the segregated reserves was the idea that the First Nations were doomed to extinction, and that the reserves were a kindness, protecting them and offering refuge from white violence, in their last days. This convenient fiction was often expressed as *smoothing the pillow of a dying race.* The capacity for the colonists to invent reasons for multiplying the damage to Aboriginal people seems to have been infinite.

Some Aboriginal people went to the reserves, willingly or unwillingly, but others didn't. My reading showed me how wrong I'd been about something else I'd always assumed: that there was uniformity about what went on. Different people were making different choices from the narrowing opportunities open to them. A reserve was set up near Werris Creek, and some of the people displaced by my great-grandfather might have gone there. But others probably stayed, patching together the best life they could in the gaps the new people allowed them, and doing whatever they could to stay on their Country.

Tom Maunder did okay for himself. Forest Farm thrived, enough for him to buy several other properties, including a big farm near Gunnedah called Rothesay. But he hadn't really chosen to come here, and right to the end of his life, when he used the word *home*, he meant England.

> Grandfather Maunder seems to have been something of a tyrant and reading between the lines it wasn't a very happy marriage. At one stage in their later years, Grandfather went back to what he called the Old Country – or home – for a trip, but his wife wouldn't go with him.

Sitting in my car at the gate of what used to be Forest Farm, looking at this landscape that says *home* to me, and thinking about my great-grandfather going to his grave calling England *home* … what does it make me feel?

On my way to Wisemans Ferry – it wasn't long after the referendum about the Voice – I'd seen a sign on someone's gate: *I'm Australian. I love this country but government and bureaucracy are f...g this country. Vote no.*

I'm remembering that sign and what I thought when I read it: if you'd been born within sound of Bow bells, like Thomas Maunder, or in Bermondsey, like Solomon Wiseman, and you objected to something your government was doing, would you feel the need to start by announcing that you belonged to the place – *I'm English* – and that you loved it? I don't think so. Surely you'd only need to do that if, deep down, you weren't convinced.

Imagine the difference, if your family really did belong. Imagine if Wiseman hadn't been caught red-handed on that dark night in 1805, and I'd been born in Bermondsey. I'd walk beside the Thames and know that my forebears had walked where I was walking – not just since 1805, but back to the Ice Ages. That they'd been there, on that stretch of land, through the Vikings coming, and Boadicea, and King Arthur, and the Romans, right up to the buzz-bombs of World War Two. That all their bodies were part of the dust I was walking on, and that when I died my dust would join them. Whether or not you knew the particular stories about particular individuals, they'd be with you at every turn of every path, a jostling crowd of family across centuries, in every crease of the land and every well-known twist of the Thames.

It would be a different way of being in the world, if you knew yourself to be spinning through eternity in the company of all those ghosts of your family. What a profound connection to your place that would give you. There'd be no sense of a murky history standing between you and your love for the land of your birth. You'd know you had every right to be there, untainted by misgivings. It would probably be unnecessary to make a big song and dance – *I'm Australian and I love my country!* – about belonging.

The man (okay, I'm assuming it was a man) who wrote that sign would no doubt bristle at the idea that he was on stolen land. He'd talk about how much he loved the place and how connected he felt to it. How his family had been on it for generations and how he'd live there for the rest of his life. It would be a brave person who'd stop the flow of his eloquence to point out that you can love something that's been stolen. Your love for it isn't in dispute. But it doesn't change the fact that it was stolen.

Growing up, I'd never felt like a proper Australian. I wasn't interested in sport, wasn't crazy about the beach, and didn't know one end of a sheep from the other. All the books I read, the poetry I loved, the pictures that shaped my imagination – they were all English. Physically I was in Australia, and physically I loved it, it was my heartland. But in some ways, England felt like home, too.

Like so many other Australians of my generation, I got myself over there as soon as I could. I refused to be a tourist – after all, I belonged there! In the five years I lived in London I never went to see the Changing of the Guard, never visited Westminster Abbey. I'd walk for miles, lost, rather than be seen on a street corner with a tourist map flapping in my hand.

But an Australian in London learns quickly that, although she might consider England her cultural home, the locals know she's something even lower than a foreigner: a colonial. It wasn't only the rude comments about my accent. It wasn't even the English woman who told me a long story about some Australians who'd pinched the ashtrays from a house they were staying in. I don't blame them, she said, they're from convict stock. It's in the genes. As an afterthought, she politely asked, And tell me, dear, do *you* have the taint?

Nothing changed even when my books were being published there. A very pukka chap organised a reading for me in Cambridge and as we walked there, he said, I asked my mother if she'd like to come to your reading. She said, An Orstralian writer? Oh darling, I don't think so. Out of misplaced courtesy I laughed along with him, though I didn't find it even a little bit funny. But you learned not to protest at English rudeness. You'd be told you had a chip on your shoulder.

It was confusing. In Australia I was one of the colonists. I was descended from the English and the Irish who'd taken the place. I wasn't proud of that, but I accepted that it was who I was. But in England I seemed almost to be the colonised: a second-class, second-hand, inferior, imitation Brit.

When I went back to England twenty years after that first trip, it was to research my convict forebear Solomon Wiseman, and to try to imagine my way into the life he'd lived as a lighterman on the Thames. Standing on the wash of stones beside that river, on the exact spot he'd been caught on that dark night stealing some Brazil wood, a lifetime's scratchiness about *where I belonged* evaporated. If not for the chance of Solomon Wiseman being caught pinching that timber, some variant of me would have grown up over the river in Bermondsey. I didn't have to *pretend* to belong to England, the way I'd pretended twenty years before. Genetically and historically, I *did* belong.

Paradoxically, that had the effect of freeing me. My whole life I'd lived with that feeling of belonging in two places and not properly belonging in either. Now all that fell away. Yes, I was connected to England in some ways. Accepting that as a given, rather than feeling that I had to labour at proving it, made things simple. But I wasn't English, and my connection to England was remote. Love it or hate it, Australia was my true and only home. The job now was to get on with working out how to be Australian. That meant working out what it meant to be descended from the people who'd taken it, acre by acre, over so many years, from the people whose place it was.

Tom Maunder selected the land and set about clearing it – hard work with nothing but an axe, a saw, and a crowbar to roll the logs away. He wouldn't have bothered clearing the strips beside the road or the leftover corners of land. And that's why, generations later, those strips and triangles are thick with something you could call *forest*: trees, bushes and tangled undergrowth all muddled together. And now and then, in among all that, are the remains of gigantic dead trees. No living trees that I've seen around here are anything like as big as these massive corpses. These, I think, might have been the ones intentionally left unburned by Gomeroi people long ago, trees that grew without competition. The majestic old corpses are the ghost of that handmade *gentleman's park*. When the traditional burning stopped, the muddled tangle grew up around them.

I'm driving slowly along the pale dusty road when, high up on the trunk of one of those dead giants, I see a scar. It's not the kind of blaze the white men made to show where their boundary was, or where the track ran. There are a few of those along this woodland road too, but they're a different shape, and they're not as high up the trunk. The white men wanted to make a mark in the easiest way, at axe-wielding height. They wanted the mark, the hole: the negative, as it were. When white men blazed a tree, it was a message: *Here's the track*, or *My land starts here.* It was a way of asserting that they'd taken it over. This is a very different kind of scar: deliberately and carefully shaped. It's more like the canoe scar back at St Albans Common, only much smaller, about a metre long. The people who made this wanted the positive, the piece of bark.

It's shaped like a fat leaf, an oval squeezed to a point at both ends. It might have been a shield or a dish. The scar starts something like two metres up the trunk. Someone had to get up off the ground to cut it out, maybe standing on someone's shoulders, or perching on some kind of ramp or ladder. But you can see why they went to that trouble – up there the bark looks fine-grained and dense. Lower down it's coarser and fibrous. A shield or dish made of that lower bark would soon crack.

Then someone had to chip and chop around the shape with an axe through a thickness of hard bark. Even with a metal axe it would have taken a while. Then there'd be the delicate business of levering it out.

I can't imagine how you'd do it, and in a way I feel it's none of my stickybeak business. What I can see is all I need to know: that this is a script recording a moment of the past, a historical document as irreplaceable and precious as any of the pieces of old paper that I've pulled on white gloves to turn through.

I photograph it as well as I can from several different angles, and when I drive on I realise similar scars are everywhere along this corner of leftover land, as if perhaps these remnant scraps of country had become the only places where cutting out a shield or dish was still possible after the coming of the white people. What that density of marks is saying – and it's unsettling to hear – is how many people lived here, and how relatively recently. This is *old* history but it's not *ancient* history. The scars on these trees might have been fresh when Maunder saw them.

I feel the need to take a photo of each one. Every grey leaf-shape is still telling its story. But for how much longer? The trees are decaying with every year, and taking those stories with them. There's an urge to record, to keep from oblivion.

I've nearly come to the end of the strip of roadside bush when I see one more. It's not a leaf-shape but a broad, roughly circular shape right below the Y of two branches, where the tree bulges in a fat comfortable curve. You can see the wide accommodating dish it would have made. I'm imagining how a woman might have used it to gather food – berries, birds' eggs, lizards, bulbs, roots – and take it back to the camp to be shared out. You'd carry it on your hip, I think. It's exactly the right size to be a comfortable fit. Carrying it like that would give you a free hand for picking or plucking or waving away the flies or holding the hand of a toddler.

I don't know any of this, of course. I'm really thinking about myself – how I'd carry that dish. Imagining it tucked against my body like that, as a physical, tactile thing, makes for something that feels true, a kind of understanding. But even as I'm feeling it, I'm thinking, perhaps I shouldn't. What do I know about any of this? That understanding – almost empathy – that I'm experiencing is an illusion, perhaps an impertinence. Still, I've felt that dish on my hip, and I can't un-feel it. In fact trying to un-feel is just another way to close down something that needs to be opened up. Feel away, I tell myself. Imagine away. Just don't mistake it for anything real.

The sun's sinking down towards the ridge and the shadows are long. I'm driving slowly towards Currabubula now, on my way back to Tamworth and the caravan park, on a stretch of dusty, potholed road. It turns a corner and dips to cross the creek. This part is dry now, just a few pools glinting among the stones. It's a lovely scene: the golden track with the dust of my passage glowing radiant in the sun, the trees arching overhead, the creek bed with its soft-looking rounded boulders. There's a perfect spot to sit on a rock beside the creek. It's so inviting that I stop and take a seat where so many others must surely have done the same.

It takes a moment for me to see that a little way off, the stones of the creek bed sparkle with broken glass from what looks like the remains of a beer-bottle-throwing competition. For years, picking up rubbish whenever I see it in the bush has been a habit. People laugh at me but I can't bear not to do it. Why? I think it's because everything I've ever tried to think about *how to be here* has always ended in old, worn-out, circular thoughts: I'm on stolen land, but I can't give it back because it's the only home I have. Cleaning one tiny speck of the vast *taken* place is meaningless, but it's been a way to do *something*, even if it was a ridiculous something. Thinking about it now, on this journey, I see that it might also have been a way of keeping that question – *how can we be here?* – active, a living question still needing to be thought about, waiting for the time when I was ready to look at it.

I picture the bottle-throwers coming back for another drinking session – *Oi, what bugger's been cleaning up?* – and hurling the next lot of bottles further, faster, harder. Cleaning up is pointless. But even as I'm seeing the picture in my mind, I'm going to the car and finding a bag, getting down into the creek bed and crouching there, picking up the broken glass. I'm hoping no one drives past, though. I don't want to be seen doing what I'm doing, as if it's dirty and shameful.

Now what's that about, when it's not me who should feel ashamed? It's because I'm part of the world that's done this and all the other damage. I don't have any urge to hurl bottles at rocks, but in a horrible way I think I understand the impulse. The bottle-hurlers are responding to the same shadow that I feel, the dragging unease that I think might live somewhere in all non-Indigenous Australians, whether or not they're aware of it. It's just that I'm writing into that feeling rather than hurling beer bottles into it.

No one comes by. I get back into the car and drive off, the bulging bag clinking its confused little song.

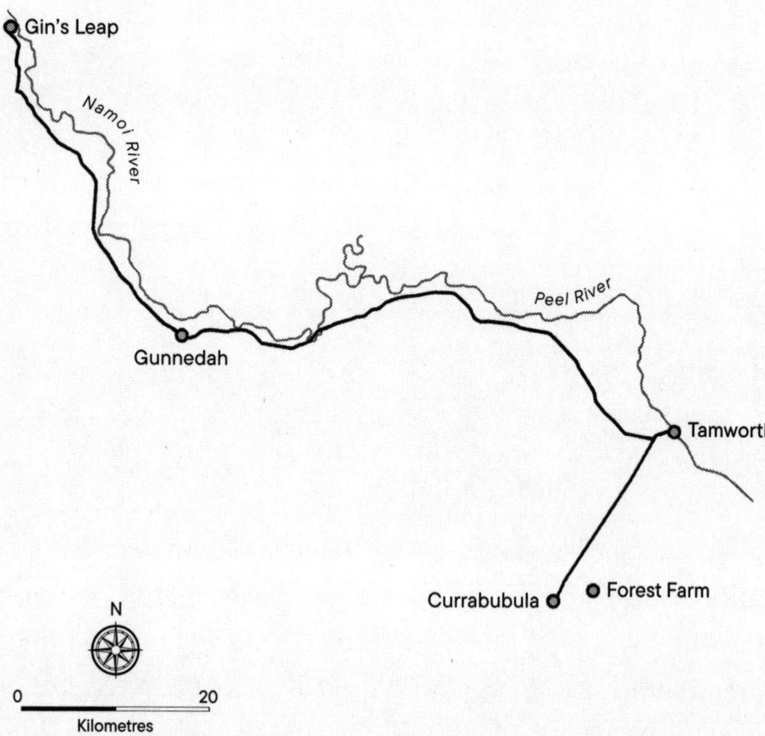

Gin's Leap
Namoi River
Gunnedah
Peel River
Tamworth
Currabubula
Forest Farm
N
0
20
Kilometres

GUNNEDAH

Thomas and Sarah Maunder had seven children. The second-youngest was my grandmother – christened Sarah Catherine like her mother and grandmother, but always called Dolly. She was born in 1881 and grew up at Forest Farm. She wanted to train as a teacher but her father stopped any thought of that. *Over my dead body any daughter of mine goes out to work!* In 1910 she married Albert Russell, a man she'd been to school with and who had come to work for her father. She was a reluctant bride but it was that or end up as an old maid. The newlyweds went to the farm near Gunnedah, 70 ks north-west of Currabubula, that Dolly's father owned. The idea was that Dolly and Bert would share-farm Rothesay for a few years and then buy it from him.

My mother was born in Gunnedah in 1912 and spent her first six years at Rothesay. She remembered it with great fondness.

I have a few early memories of Rothesay – it seems to me now to have been a big house – certainly there was one very big room which must have been the kitchen-living room because I remember the stove and a huge kitchen table – there was a beautiful white cedar tree outside the window, which I loved.

If I have a paradise which I lost as most people seem to, it would be those early years on the farm. My elder brother Frank and I must have been almost like twins, with barely eighteen months between us – one morning very early Frank and I were outside – I can still remember how fresh and lovely it was that morning. The house was on a small hill and we could run down towards the river, but I don't remember the river – it must have been a fair distance because we had a well and we wouldn't have needed a well if the river was handy, would we? I remember Dad going down the well to fix it in some way and I was terrified that he would die down there because I'd been told about miners and their (especially then) dangerous occupation. I can remember the river overflowing, coming near the house and feeling frightened because the grown-ups seemed to be frightened.

I remember too the unbelievably lovely smell of rain on dry soil – a country child must know from early on the drama of droughts and floods – the seasons never lose their power and influence.

Twenty years ago, as part of the research for the book about my mother, I got in touch with the people who owned Rothesay. They were warm and welcoming. They invited me to lunch, showed me everything, let me spend time mooching around. I saw the old well – bricked up now – that Bert had gone down. I stood on the verandah looking down towards the river and tried to imagine it in flood. The owners and I discussed what a white cedar looked like, and was that one over there?

On that visit I was thinking about my mother, my Uncle Frank, my grandmother, my grandfather. It seemed important to stand where they'd stood and see something close to what they saw. It was a way of telling Mum's story as truthfully as I could, even though I had to imagine parts of it.

But today I'm heading from Tamworth to Gunnedah for something different. It's broader than standing in the footprints of my forebears, and I don't need to bother the hospitable folk at Rothesay again. Instead, I'm looking out for what my narrow focus that day didn't allow me to take in: the big picture. To feel the whole landscape, not just the house that stands in it.

Gunnedah is a pleasant small town by the river and today it seems a place of no verticals, ironed by the sun onto the great flatness all around it. Past the town I turn off on a side road. When I find a spot to stop I pull over and stand on the doorsill of the car so I can see into the distance.

The flatness of this landscape is remarkable. I feel the need to keep looking right and left to check that, yes, it seems as level as a table as far as the eye can see. There was plenty of flat land around Goonoo Goonoo and Piallaway. But it wasn't like this. In those places, the plains were bounded by hills. Here nothing stops the eye. It looks out and out and out and finally at the end of vision, land bleeds into sky.

The *explorers* knew a bit about soil – that was why they were *exploring* – and they'd have recognised this as the best: a dark, friable loam, the colour of chocolate and just as rich. You could grow anything in it. And no hills, no gullies – easy going for those men with their bullocks and drays, and easy later for other men with ploughs.

And what I'm understanding, peering out into the endless space, is that this open country is perfect for horses. Everywhere else I've been, at Piallaway and Forest Farm and before that down on the Hunter and the Hawkesbury, there are places where people on foot could get away from people on horses, up on the steep slopes covered with loose stone and scrub. But here there's nowhere to hide. Out here a man on a horse could outpace the strongest man on foot. A few men on a few horses could round up a whole group of other humans.

You could be with your family in a place that had always been yours, and up till now had been safe, some creek-side spot among a few trees. Somewhere else – miles away perhaps – white men had lost some sheep to an Aboriginal cooking-fire, or a shepherd had been attacked. The people who'd eaten the sheep or speared the shepherd might have had nothing to do with you, but the white men weren't always fussy about whom they punished. You'd be asleep, the sun not yet risen. You'd hear shouts and wake up to find yourself surrounded by men on horses with guns. There'd be nowhere to hide and nowhere to run from the horses. The guns did the killing, but the horses did the chasing-down.

I've read about how horses *gave the colonists an advantage*. But, perched up on the doorsill with my hat jammed down against the glare, I seem to be working it out all over again from first principles.

I *feel* it now: the vulnerability of all those folk on foot. How it would be to have those huge alien creatures rushing at you, rearing up, with a man pointing his gun down at you, and running, running, running, till you stumbled and fell.

Visualising that, I'm thinking about First Nations people stealing horses and guns and using them against the invaders, the way Native Americans did. It happened here too, though not on a big scale. But it's not part of our stereotype of how First Nations people fought back. Many non-Indigenous Australians, even now, refuse to name what happened on the frontier as a war, and that's partly because of the weapons Aboriginal people mostly used – spears, fire, attacks on stock and crops. That did plenty of damage, but in some minds, conflict like that can't be given the status of war.

Aboriginal people stole guns and ammunition in raids on homesteads. At times, escaped convicts helped them. The warriors used guns effectively and understood them well enough to repair them. On occasion they even stole lead and melted it down to make shot.

But for many reasons, guns and horses didn't become a big part of Aboriginal warfare. Mostly it was lack of time: Native Americans had nearly three centuries – from the coming of the Spanish – to adapt to the new weapons, whereas here everything happened much more quickly. Mass deaths by epidemics overwhelmed Aboriginal people from the earliest days. And the colonists worked hard to keep guns – and even an understanding of how they worked – from Aboriginal people for as long as they could. The first governor gave an order that no gun was ever to be loaded where an Aboriginal person could watch it being done, because he thought part of the fearsome power of the gun was its mystery. There might, too, have been an obstinate distaste among some Aboriginal people for using the white man's horrible weapons and their alien animals, a philosophical or spiritual refusal.

Aboriginal use of guns was too small-scale to make much real difference to the outcome of frontier conflict. But what I'm interested in is that guns haven't been any part of the conventional non-Indigenous picture of Aboriginal warfare. The picture is of naked men with spears. I'm wondering now if that was just an oversight – or that maybe we've resisted the image of Aboriginal warriors with guns for a reason.

Guns are what our own warriors use. We're taught to respect our soldiers, even admire them, and their guns are part of their heroic mystique. If our picture of Aboriginal warfare included guns, their warriors would suddenly start to look more like our own. We'd have a cultural template to recognise them for what they indubitably were: patriots defending their homelands. And we couldn't go on refusing to name what went on as a war.

One of the favourite games of my generation of kids was Cowboys and Indians. We got our material from Hollywood and books like *The Last of the Mohicans*. Being a cowboy was fun because you got to have a gun and go Blam! Blam! Being an Indian was pretty good too. You could do a lot of whooping and throw yourself into a drawn-out elaborate death.

I'm thinking about all that now, looking out over this uncompromising plain. We never thought – well, how could we? We were only kids – about what had happened to flesh-and-blood men and women and children when real cowboys met real Indians. The films and the books and the countless gangs of kids playing at killing each other – from our perspective now it's horrifying, trivialising a vast human tragedy. The history was distorted, belittled, sentimentalised. But at least it was known that there'd been a war between the Europeans and the First Nations in America. That most basic fact of American history was known to every child who ever played the game.

But for us Australian kids, Cowboys and Indians was unmistakably from somewhere else, and there were no games about "Settlers and Aborigines". We didn't think of ourselves as having had anything like a war – in fact we hardly knew that Aboriginal people had fought back at all. Where that knowledge should have been was a blank place in our picture of ourselves.

Or was it? Was our enthusiasm for Cowboys and Indians a displacement of something our society *did* know, at a level too deeply buried to be recognised? Did the story from someone else's past give us a way of circling the darkness at the heart of our own?

At the time Dolly and Bert came to Gunnedah in 1910 that darkness hadn't ended, it was just taking a different form. By then the business of reserves had shifted. The new ones were mostly not initiated by Aboriginal people, and they were now so tightly controlled by the Aborigines Protection Board that they were essentially prisons. Some were church missions, but whatever they were called, and whoever ran them, the people who lived there needed written permission from the manager – always white – to take a job, to get married, or to leave the reserve. The independent Aboriginal farms were revoked. The farmers were removed, and the now much-improved land was taken by settlers.

The noose had to be tightened because, although the pillow had been *smoothed*, the *dying race* was still going strong. The so-called *full-bloods* were fewer, but when the officials did a count they were alarmed at the growing numbers of people of mixed heritage.

Part of the job of the reserves now was to stop that trend, and the new policy was to *breed out the colour*. One method was to control who married whom – hence the requirement for permission to marry. Another was to remove light-skinned children and make them part of the white world, so they'd lose any sense of being Aboriginal. If they went on to have children, the idea was that they'd have them with a white partner. Their children would hardly be black at all! *Home-finders* were employed by the reserves to persuade parents to send their children away to dormitories and so-called training institutions. If persuasion didn't work, the board could remove a child they said was *orphaned* or *neglected*. They didn't have to bring any evidence forward and there was no appeal.

It's not surprising that many Aboriginal people steered clear of the reserves if they could, and went on living an improvised, embattled life on the fringes of the white world, supporting themselves in whatever ways they could. Men like my grandfather would have needed men now and then to help him plough and harvest. Women like my grandmother would have needed help with housework and childcare. But the family stories are silent about any of that.

I'm in need of a cup of tea and a sandwich, and like every other human in this dry landscape, I'm drawn to the water. On the outskirts of Gunnedah I find a big park on a bend of the river. It's another lovely spot: a big, soft crescent of level ground – it's probably under water when the river floods – and those huge comforting trees that I think are river red gums. The river is low at the moment, way down between steep banks, and a murky brown. I wonder if it was always this colour. So much clearing and ploughing, all that wheat, all that cotton, so many dams, so much irrigation. I've read that the now-muddy Hawkesbury was as clear as a pane of glass until the colonists arrived and cleared along its banks. In the past this river, too, was probably clear and full of fish, a place of generous plenty for the people who lived here.

There's no one else here and I'm looking forward to strolling along the bank in the dappled shade. I'm all set up on the picnic table with my thermos, I've drowned the teabag in the hot water and I'm opening the little thing of milk. I've been here – what, five minutes? – when a yellow car appears, driving slowly, at the entrance to the park. I squint up at it – the crescent of level land I'm on is surrounded by a ridge of high ground, and the car has stopped on the crest of the ridge, pointing down towards me.

A man gets out. He's a hundred metres away, but I can see he's a young bloke with a baseball cap that puts his face in shadow. Now another bloke gets out from the passenger side. They both stand looking down towards me. The passenger has his hands on his hips. And now suddenly there's another vehicle, a bigger, blockier, black, shiny kind of thing that's come up a side track and it's also stopped on the top of the ridge a bit further along. No one gets out, but I can hear the engine, that low diesel growl.

The blokes in the yellow car are having a conversation over the bonnet. I can't hear what they're saying but I hear them laugh. A big loud laugh. What you might call a performative laugh. The driver stretches, his arms go up, and I realise he's taking off his cap, and now he's taking off his t-shirt. Tosses the t-shirt into the cab, puts the cap back on with a decisive flick. Settles it at the back of his head, a man taking his time. He stands bare-chested, watching me. The other one is fiddling with his pants and now he's in the man-having-a-piss stance. He's not hiding or even turning away. I can see a line of sparkle.

Bugger the tea, bugger the sandwich. I pour the tea out on the ground, pile everything back in the bag. Get into the car and – I've never done this before and I have to work out where it is – press the button that locks all the doors.

The yellow car isn't quite blocking the track, but I'm going to have to squeeze past it. Or should I drive around the park? There might be another way out. But what if I get stuck in this soft ground, or cornered somewhere?

They must have seen me turn off the road and bump along the track. They saw I was a woman, on my own. I shouldn't have come here. My heart seems to be beating in the wrong place, it's come up into my throat. I feel a kind of shivery thing around my shoulders. This lovely place is suddenly a trap. The sunlight has become lurid, with a nasty yellowey quality. The shadows cast by the great thick tree trunks are solid black and they're confusing, making it hard to see clearly and think clearly. I'm trying to slow down my mind because actually I'm not thinking very well, I've got steady thoughts but each thought has a halo or radiance of the opposite of calm. Actually, what it is is fear.

I'm driving up the track, briskly but not rushing. I've put the sun visor down. That feels better, but how ridiculous. As if a sun visor's going to protect me! I'm keeping my eyes very carefully on the road and I'm driving very steadily, I won't slow down or speed up or do anything that could make me skid or stall.

The one having a piss has joined his mate on the driver's side. That's good. They're now both on the other side from where I have to pass them. They're staring at me. The big glossy black thing hasn't moved. The windows are tinted black so I can't see through them, but someone's in there, watching me.

As I get up next to the yellow car, passing it not too slowly, not too fast, there's a big bang and something jumps in my chest. In spite of myself I glance around. The one with his shirt off has banged his hand on the bonnet of his car. It's made a puff of dust. He's holding his hand up to show me – he's going to do it again. I can see his face now, under his baseball cap, and his teeth. You could say he was smiling, but there's nothing friendly about it. He's pleased I got a fright. He bangs again, but I'm ready for it this time and I'm past, going faster now because I'm thinking, What about the black car, what if it comes over the other track and cuts me off?

They let me go. In the rear-view mirror I can see the two beside the yellow car standing hands on hips, watching me drive away. Whoever's in the black one is still invisible behind the opaque windows, but he'd be watching me too.

GIN'S LEAP

Looking at the map before I came, a name caught my eye, a place about 45 ks north-west of Gunnedah called Gin's Leap. It's a name out of an only-recently-past Australia in which it was quite ordinary to call an Aboriginal woman a *gin*. I wondered how such a dismissive put-down of a term could still appear on any map today.

And I was curious. Who was the woman, and why had she leaped? There was nothing about Gin's Leap in the family stories, but I was on this trip to see what standing on a place could tell me, so I thought I'd go and look.

Gin's Leap turns out to be a sheer cliff as high as a skyscraper, part of a mighty bulge of rock that towers over the flatness all around. Like Uluru, it's an extraordinary anomaly on the landscape, a freak of geology. I stand beneath it, looking up at the massive bulk of stone, ragged in some parts and rather horribly smooth in others. It's a sunny midday, but being under that gigantic mass of rock feels solemn, oppressive, a bit spooky.

It's the name, I suppose. It tells you that something bad happened here.

The sign put up by the shire, a jaunty purple thing, tells the story:

> The origins of this historical natural monument follow the tragic death of a pair of ill-fated young Aboriginal lovers, a modern day Romeo and Juliet. The girl, promised to an elder of her tribe, ran away with a young Aboriginal man. Hotly pursued by Gamaroi tribesmen, the lovers jumped to their deaths from somewhere along the top of the rock.

Once the story gets to Romeo and Juliet it hits its stride. It knows that story and speaks with confidence. But it takes a weird, tentative, roundabout route to get there: *The origins of this historical natural monument follow the tragic death* ... First up, this isn't a *monument* – a manmade thing memorialising something. And how can something be *historical* and also *natural*? The *origins* of this thing are actually in geology. And if they're an *origin*, they don't *follow* anything. There's a sense of terrific strain about that opening, as if a committee has met and had difficulty thrashing out the exact words. People have added, other people have subtracted, there's been a bit of heat around the table, and what you get adds up to no real sense.

But it's not the grammar that makes me look sideways at the story. There's a place in Queensland called The Leap, where some white men on horses harried a group of Aboriginal people up a mountain and forced them over the edge to their deaths. Thea Astley wrote a famous novel about it, based on the historical record. So when I read this sentimental, romantic tale, my first thought was, Pull the other one. For a start, if two lovers – not just the woman – leaped voluntarily to their deaths, wouldn't it have been called something like *Lovers' Leap*? Straight away that points to something fuzzy.

Gin is the word for *woman* in the Dharug language. But when it was borrowed by the colonists it took on a demeaning and sexualised vibe, because the people who borrowed it were only interested in Aboriginal women for sex. Yes, a *gin* leaping off this cliff might have been in love with the wrong man. But the picture that comes to my mind is that she was being chased by a white man who wanted her. Chased, and she preferred death to the white man's embrace. Or said no, and made the man angry enough to force her over the edge.

Some people drive up, get out, take a few photographs. An older couple, they stand for a long time looking up at the cliff face, now shadowed and sombre. They're talking quietly, though I can't hear what they're saying. The woman points – was it *there*? – and the man points to another place along that awful edge. Then they stand in silence, looking up.

This is an immensely powerful, singular, spiritual place. This woman and man feel it, as everyone must who comes here. The first strangers who saw it – *explorers* or *squatters* – surely they'd have felt it too. They probably thought there'd be Aboriginal stories about it, and they might have wanted to know them. In their world, if you wanted to know something, you assumed you had the right to ask, and to expect an answer. In other worlds, knowledge is a precious and sacred thing. It's only shared with people who've been initiated into its importance and who will value it properly. Outsiders might be gauche enough to ask, but they won't be told.

I imagine the white men standing where I'm standing, feeling the awe I'm feeling. What are the stories about this place, they'd have asked. No Aboriginal person was going to share any sacred knowledge with them. But one of them might have known enough about the white men to guess what kind of story would satisfy them. Oh, it's like *Romeo and Juliet*, he might have said, and watched the white man believe him.

After so long, it may be that no one can prove exactly what happened at Gin's Leap. But oh, what a useful thing the *Romeo and Juliet* story is. We – white people – all know it and as soon as we read those words our sentimental feelings about Shakespeare's lovers flow in quickly, appealingly, to fill the place where we want a story. This one's rich and familiar. We don't need to go looking for another.

But did First Nations cultures have our obsession with romantic love, the kind that makes young lovers kill themselves? The notion is so deeply ingrained in Western culture that it's easy to assume it's universal, but it mightn't be.

In my twenties I went to India and was shocked at the fact of arranged marriages – even more shocked when several young women explained that it worked well, and they were very happy in theirs. No one had unrealistic expectations: if romantic love happened, that was a bonus, but it wasn't what marriage was about.

Marriage was about two people with similar values and backgrounds making a solid relationship. It was like a good business partnership, where there was mutual respect and the affection of sharing an enterprise – the enterprise of making a family. I could see that these young women thought that the ephemera of sexual attraction, or the puffed-up feverishness of romantic love, were poor ways to choose a life partner. When I argued, they politely pointed to the high rates of marriage breakdown in my system.

So – I don't know enough about First Nations societies to know how the system of promising young girls to a man worked out in practice. But I do know that arranged marriages aren't necessarily the horror that romance-centred Western culture assumes they are. Maybe there were young men and women willing to die for love, but I'm open to the possibility that there weren't. Whatever the truth is, citing star-crossed lovers here is useful if you want to cover up any of the nastier things that might have happened.

It does another bit of heavy lifting, too. Embedded in it is criticism of the way First Nations people did things: how cruel, to promise a young girl to an older man! If the story has a villain, it's the tribal laws about marriage.

If you wanted to believe that *the blacks* were an inferior race, savage and barbaric, not quite as human as you, then this story would be convincing. And once you were convinced, the next step would be to feel no guilt and no responsibility for doing what was done. If they were barbaric and cruel towards each other, the thinking would go, doesn't that make our barbarism and cruelty towards them appropriate, justifiable – even inevitable?

In spite of the *Romeo and Juliet* overlay, I suspect the story contains a remnant of truth. This geological extravagance could be called something cheerful or emotionally neutral – *Sublime Peak* or *The Walls of Jericho*. But the story attached to it has a thread of violence and fear and despair, connected to sex. It's as if the truth is obstinately refusing to be erased – as if, along with the propensity for violence, hatred, bigotry and lies, in the muddle of things that make up human beings there's also some tough thread of honesty. It was so easy to make bad things disappear in the olden days. Many of them *were* disappeared. But in some places – and I think Gin's Leap could be one of them – there's a ghost of truth, a fleck of the real, running along through the lies.

TAMWORTH

The next bit of family story happened in Tamworth, 75 ks east of Gunnedah, and I'm heading back there now. There's not much to see as I speed along, only enormous squared-off paddocks where the crops grow neatly into every corner, edge to edge, a uniform coating laid over the land. The highway is edged with white fluff, spillover from the trucks taking cotton to market. People don't grow wheat so much out here these days – the big money's in cotton for the t-shirts of the world.

Gin's Leap has got me looking askance at the surface of things. Names especially. Where they come from, what they mean, what happens when you take them apart.

There's *Heatherbrae* as I flash past. *Blairgowrie. Glen Something.* That was people trying to pretend they weren't here, foreigners hungry for home. It's insulting, when you think about it. You're wishing the place was somewhere else. You've come by this bit of land, and now you're going to honour it by giving it the name of the place you actually love, the place that's a real place, not this eerie dry country where you don't really, in your heart of hearts, want to be.

Smithvale. Hordernvale. That's people naming the place after themselves. Some of those early colonists would never have dreamed of being able to own land back in Britain. Solomon Wiseman, living a hard hungry life in London, was one of those. As well as attaching his name to the area around the ferry, he also established a short-lived village called *Solomonville*, up on the plateau of the Great North Road.

You can understand the impulse. Owning land must have seemed a gift from God. And if enough people told each other that Aboriginal people didn't have a word for property, didn't use the land except to wander over it foraging whatever they could, and above all that they were a lower form of human – well, you might let yourself feel entitled to give it your own name. There'd be no mistake then, and no giving it back. But unlike the *Heatherbrae* people, serene in their nostalgia, it seems the *Smithvale* people needed to shout about the place being theirs.

There's a run of bland ones – *Fairview*, *Hilltop*, *Tall Trees*. In my present frame of mind they seem almost ostentatiously noncommittal. They're not looking back to where they came from, and they're not quite ready to look forward to the future in which generations of Smiths and Horderns will live on the place that carries their name. They're reducing the past and future to nothing more than the present moment, the visible facts in front of them. There's a *fair view*. There's a *hill top*. There are a lot of *tall trees*. There's no history here. Day one is now. That view. That hill. Those trees.

And what about the Aboriginal words on some of those gates: *Yarragindi*, *Mandamulla*, *Moolawong*? What does it mean to give your place an Aboriginal name? Is it respectful, an acknowledgement of Country right there on your front gate? You can tell people, Oh, it means such-and-such. You know the story behind the word, the story behind the place. That gives you a connection to it.

And that's where it gets a bit slippery. Context is all, and back in the nineteenth century, when these homesteads were established and named, the context was the colonists' sense of entitlement: that the land was open for the taking, and if the taking had to be done by violence, so be it.

In that context, naming your place *Moolawong* starts to look more like appropriation than acknowledgement. You've borrowed someone else's ownership by borrowing their word. You've glossed over the way ownership has passed from them to you. You're establishing continuity rather than rupture by pasting the rupture over with this thin slip of continuity. And you're pointing to something that's gone, like putting a blue plaque on a house in England to tell people that once upon a time Charles Dickens lived there. The plaque says, *It was a long time ago and he doesn't live here anymore.*

My first boyfriend lived in a suburb of Sydney called Wahroonga. He told me that the word meant *our home* in the local language. I didn't query it back then. Now I'm remembering it with a flinch. I'll ask you what you call it, and you'll explain that it's *our home*. Then I'll take it as *our* home, and call it that – but in your language.

And what about the house I saw in a seaside village near Sydney called *Didjabringyagrogalong*. Now that's not slippery, that's thumbing your nose.

I don't know what people should call their places. But what I do know is that when you call your property *Moolawong*, you're doing something that bristles with unconscious meanings.

And now I'm wondering exactly how those names were arrived at. How did the settlers know the words in the first place?

Let's imagine a squatter there with his sheep. He's decided on a few creeks and ridgelines as his boundaries and he's got a hut up. Then one night he's sitting staring into the fire with the mug of tea in his hand, watching the suave flow and flicker of flames around the sticks, and he's thinking, What will I call this new place of mine? When I send away to apply for the depasturing licence, what name will I give it? Oh, Major Mitchell said it was called Moolawong. I'll call it that.

The *explorer* Mitchell is famous for giving Aboriginal names to places, as he gave Currabubula its name. Until recently I thought that was a mark of someone a bit progressive, perhaps even a bit respectful, putting some nuance of acknowledgement into the stark picture of invasion. Then I read that he did it for the most practical of reasons – so that when the next *explorer* came along and asked the local people what the place was called, he'd realise it was the same one Mitchell had already been through. It had nothing to do with acknowledgement and everything to do with efficiency.

I'm drawing a picture of it for myself. There's the man in boots and hat, standing in the sun with the Aboriginal man. Behind the man in boots is a group of other men in boots and hats, sitting up high on their horses. Behind the men and the horses there's a dray piled high with things under a sheet of canvas. Someone's probably got a gun, ready loaded. He's holding it down at his side, out of sight. It's for just-in-case. The man in boots gestures around, a big fluid movement of the arm to take in the landscape. *What name?*

There might be another Aboriginal man with him. In my primary school textbooks the explorers often had a *native guide*, usually called *Jacky-Jacky* if he had a name at all. If there's a *Jacky-Jacky* there with the others, it's because the white men think he'll know the language of the place they've come to. He might, though not necessarily. The white men's assumption would be like bringing a Bulgarian along because you're sure he'll be able to translate when you get to Spain.

One way or another a question was asked, and something came back that was taken to be an answer. And maybe it was. The Aboriginal man might have understood the question, and he might have been prepared to give the answer.

But it's also possible that he mightn't have wanted to share the name of his place with this stranger. What business was it of his? If he was so ignorant of the place that he had to ask, did he have a right to know? So he might tell the Jacky-Jacky man, Bugger that, tell him, *Slap your bum!* Jacky-Jacky understands what he's said, and turns with a straight face to the man in boots. He repeats the final bit of the answer and tells the man in boots that it's the name of the place. And forever after, it was a nice joke that the white people would never guess at, that one of them had called his place *Slap Your Bum*, up in big letters on his front gate.

These days, suburbs, libraries and sports fields are being relabelled with First Nations names. Many of us can now rattle off the original name of the area where we live. Australia Post has even given us a booklet so we can address our letters with both the English name and the First Nations one.

Is that any different, morally any less ambiguous, than an Aboriginal word on a country gate? I think it is, because the context is different. Every year it becomes harder not to know what happened here. The First Nations names are a gesture towards acknowledging the insults and exclusions of the past.

Or is it nothing more than indulgence in what a witty politician of my youth called *the politics of the warm inner glow*? A meaningless thing to make us feel we've done something? Perhaps even that we've done enough, when we actually haven't done anything at all?

Yes, there might be some truth in that too.

Australia has a long history of white people pretending to be Aboriginal, the way the names on those gates are pretending. The writer Sreten Bozic was one. He was Serbian, but he adopted the pen name B. Wongar and allowed people to think that he was of Aboriginal descent. His dozen books draw on his knowledge of Aboriginal life and culture in a way that kept the ambiguity going.

But the most extraordinary of the many stories of fakery is that of Elizabeth Durack. She was the granddaughter of a squatter who took an enormous area of the Kimberley from the Miriuwung and Gajerrong people and made a fortune. Elizabeth's sister Mary wrote books about their lives there, the most famous triumphantly titled

Kings in Grass Castles. Elizabeth painted for many years without her art finding much recognition, then late in life she began to make paintings of a different sort. She exhibited and sold them as the work of an old Aboriginal man, Eddie Burrup. She entered fully into the fiction she'd created, inventing a biography and personality for Eddie. The paintings were included in exhibitions of Aboriginal art.

When the truth came out, Elizabeth Durack was unrepentant – in fact, not unrepentant as much as oblivious. She didn't get what the fuss was about. She protested that she'd grown up in the Kimberley, she knew the Aboriginal people who'd worked for her family. She spoke their language! What was wrong with inventing an Aboriginal man and putting his name to her work?

I've never pretended to be of Aboriginal descent, or invented an Aboriginal alter ego, but thinking about Streten Bozic and Elizabeth Durack, I'm remembering a certain event from my youth that I've always thought of as nothing more than a foolhardy adventure. Now I'm seeing it as something else too.

When I was about ten our family went on a car tour of the then-new Snowy Mountains Scheme. My memory is mostly of driving in the thick brown dust of the car in front. But Mum and Dad heard about a subdivision of house-sized blocks of land at Lake Eucumbene, and they bought one. From then on, every school holidays we drove from Sydney, camped on the block, and built a bit more house.

One summer four or five years after we started holidaying at the lake, I had a friend along and she and I spent our days roaming around the area. It had been a sheep run, so there were paddocks with the tussocky grass of the area, and hillsides of bush.

The big drama was about snakes. We saw red-bellied blacks, and there were probably others we never saw. My parents gave us strict instructions about how to avoid them and what to do if we came across any. We even had a pouch with a razor blade and Condy's crystals, the 1960s treatment for snake bite. But my friend and I thought we were old enough to do something more interesting than avoid snakes. We decided to go hunting for them. A local boy made us a thing he called a "snake charmer" – a long, whippy flail made of doubled-over fencing wire – and we set off with it one day towards a paddock where we'd seen snakes.

What did we think we were doing? We weren't really thinking, just looking for something exciting to do. But remembering it now, I know that in the back of my mind, if not my friend's, was a notion that we were doing what Aboriginal people had done. I'd read that they hunted snakes, cooked them and ate them. We weren't inventing an Aboriginal man and pretending to be him, but in a small way we were doing what Elizabeth Durack did: inhabiting what we thought were Aboriginal ways. Here, on land where – we assumed – Aboriginal people no longer cooked and ate snakes, we took over that role. Sixty years later I can see that, at an unconscious level, we were making ourselves the inheritors. *It was yours, and now it's ours.*

We did succeed in killing a snake. We skinned it – easier said than done – and made a fire and cooked it. My friend wouldn't come at eating it. In fact, sensible girl, she'd been against the whole snake-hunting thing from the beginning. But I ate a bit of the snake. I expected it to taste strange and horrible. In fact, the flavour and slightly greasy texture reminded me of nothing so much as a nice lamb chop.

Which, in the context of what happened on the frontier, is interesting. Aboriginal people often killed the settlers' sheep. Sometimes they left them to rot, as a message, but they ate plenty of them too. It now occurs to me that the taste might have reminded the people who ate that mutton or lamb of nothing so much as a nice length of snake. The white men's snakes had four legs and were covered with fuzzy stuff, but they tasted right. In taste, at least, they were a version of traditional food. That – as well as the fact that they'd displaced traditional food – made them fair game. But how could the new people, the non-Indigenous Australians, begin to understand?

Every time I write "non-Indigenous Australian" I think, Isn't there a better word? It's long-winded, clunky, awkward in the mouth. Maybe that's as it should be. Maybe it should be an effort to say, as it should be an effort to think about. Nothing too slick.

But there's something wrong with it because it's not an identity. It's a non-identity, a negative, an emptiness. The reason is that we haven't thought we needed a name. We take it for granted that we're the norm. *Just ordinary Australian*, you hear people say, as if it's only people who aren't the norm who need a special word for themselves. But we need to name ourselves, and be named by others, because we're not blanks and we're not the default from which everyone else is an aberration.

Richard Wiseman's generation might have called themselves *natives*, but that won't do these days. What about *whitefeller*? That's neat and easy to say, but plenty of non-Indigenous Australians aren't actually white. The bigger problem is that it suggests a kind of equivalence. Blackfeller, whitefeller, and only the skin colour is different. But we're not equivalent. Our histories and our life experiences have made differences, and skin colour is the least significant of them.

There's a bit of appropriation going on in *whitefeller*, too. *Blackfeller* has a friendly, jokey, familiar sort of vibe. It's what one *blackfeller* might call another. Flipping it over is borrowing some of that vibe, when in the world of *blackfellers*, there hasn't ever been much that was friendly or benign about *whitefellers*.

Settlers or *colonists* – that suggests there's nothing problematic about being a settler or a colonist. It leapfrogs over the thing that happened right before the settling and the colonising: the taking. And again, it doesn't sit right with someone who's recently arrived from Vietnam or Lebanon. I've been trying out *foreigners* and *strangers*. That's got the right feel, to my ears – disrupting that sense of ourselves being the norm – but it doesn't work beyond the first generation of colonists. *Invader* is correct for that first generation, too, but a conversation that starts with that probably isn't going to go anywhere very useful.

In parts of Australia the word *gubba* is sometimes used (mostly by First Nations people) for non-Indigenous Australians, especially white ones. It comes from *government man* and the word carries the whole ugly weight of what government men and whites in general have done to First Nations people in the past. The dictionary notes that it's derogatory. Like *invader*, it's not likely to catch on among the descendants of those government men.

First Nations languages have words for us. *Kartiya*, *Migaloo*,

Madjela and others. But each of those words is from the language of a different group of people. If we use one, it disregards all the other languages and the people who speak them.

In New Zealand, non-Indigenous New Zealanders (now there's a mouthful) are commonly called *pakeha*, a Maori word that signifies *non-Maori*. There are different theories about where the word comes from. One is that it's a Maori borrowing of *porker*, referring to the English sealers who left pigs behind to multiply as a food supply for future voyages. Another suggests that it might mean *white maggots*. I suppose for that reason there are people who aren't happy to be called *pakeha*, but the word is used by many people.

Embedded in the word – at least if it derives from *porker* – is the truth that non-Indigenous New Zealanders are from somewhere else. They, or their forebears, are recent arrivals. There's a respectfulness in the fact that they're prepared to accept that identity. They're using a word from their own language that's been taken and reshaped as part of the language of the place to which they're the newcomers.

In parts of northern Australia, some Aboriginal people use the word *balanda* for people who aren't Indigenous. As *pakeha* is for Maori people, *balanda* is a word borrowed by Aboriginal people that's become part of their language. It's borrowed from the Macassans – people from an island to our north who, for centuries before Europeans came here, visited the top part of Australia in certain seasons. They'd been colonised by the Dutch, and the Macassans borrowed and adapted the word the Dutch used for themselves: Hollander. So *balanda*, like *pakeha*, is a borrowing of a borrowing that's become part of First Nations languages.

I don't suppose it'll fly with my fellow non-Indigenous Australians, and I can see the problems with it, but I might experiment with thinking of myself as a *balanda.* A descendant of foreigners, using a word that's been adapted by the people who are from here, to describe my lot.

~

So here I am, a balanda coming into the town of Tamworth.

This is where the family story my mother told me connects with Tamworth:

> At Rothesay Dad grew wheat and for seven years in succession saw the crop ruined – they didn't ever get a crop. It'd be either hail or drought, or a terrific storm would flatten it just when it was ready for harvesting. I think the hail was the last straw. Mum always said it was a bumper crop – the ears bending over, full of wheat almost ready for harvesting. You can imagine the heartbreak.
>
> I can still see Mum – I couldn't have been more than five then – banging away at a saucepan on the stove. "I'm not going to stay, we're going, we're going!" She must have nagged so hard that they left.
>
> We left Gunnedah in my sixth year. That was 1918, July or August. I can remember Dad sitting me on the kitchen table and dressing me and putting on my shoes. It seems now to be night but as we went out the gate for the last time in the buggy it was daylight and I can hear Mum saying, "Goodbye, Rothesay, and I hope I never see you again." And she didn't.

> They decided to go into business and for the next ten years they bought and sold businesses, mainly hotels, and made a fortune.
>
> We will never know what made them decide to buy the Caledonian Hotel in Tamworth at the end of those ten years, but I think now it would have been a mixture of nostalgia for the area where they were born, Currabubula, and a longing to show their childhood friends and relations how well they had done in the world.

Tamworth is a medium-sized town some 75 ks east of Gunnedah. Major Mitchell saw the spot a day or two after he'd gone through the gap in the range at Currabubula. It's on a substantial river, the best source of permanent water for a long way in every direction, and it sits at the junction of the two major routes west and north. Which tells you that before it was a town, it was probably a good place for Gomeroi people too. Depending on the season and their movements, they might have been here when Mitchell came. They might have watched him coming across the plain towards them.

There's a small sign on the road coming into town: *Welcome to Kamilaroi Country.* But what the brochures in the Information Centre want you to get excited about is that Tamworth is the centre of country music in Australia. The big thing, the place where everyone goes to have their photo taken, is the Big Guitar.

Mum was fifteen when her parents bought the Caledonian, in 1927. She remembered it as all things grand.

> The Caledonian – the Cally, as most people called it – had been started by Mrs Trim about 1870, you may remember we had a few old spoons with Trim on them. It was a comfortable, well-loved hotel, the leading hotel in Tamworth. Yes, it was four shillings to have meal there. That was a lot of money, when you could have a good meal at the Greek's for ninepence.
>
> Bar trade was good and the house was full every night. This was the time when people discovered the freedom that a car gave and everyone went on trips.
>
> A lot of the furniture was made from Northern Rivers cedar but there were some other lovely pieces from England. There were beautiful glass-fronted bookcases with cupboards underneath, elegant chaises longues and armchairs, and fireplaces everywhere, of course, with wonderful fire dogs that people kept wanting to buy.
>
> The laundry was a world in itself. You can imagine the sheets to be boiled, the tablecloths and table napkins to be starched and ironed. Everything was white in those days. There were mangles, wringers, tubs, coppers, huge tables for ironing and folding, and of course everything done by hand.
>
> Part of the huge backyard was given over to "sample rooms". These were like small halls where the commercial travellers set out their samples to entice the businessmen of Tamworth

to buy. C.T.A. members stayed at the Cally at a reduced rate.

I have never seen anything like the Cally – I wish I had appreciated it more. Most sins are those of omission.

I'd been in Tamworth in 2012, researching that part of my mother's life, and top of my list of things to see was, of course, the Cally. I'd seen old photos of the place, a classic Australian pub: two storeys, French doors opening onto a wide verandah over the street, iron lace top and bottom. It took up most of a block and projected a sense of solid prosperity.

In my innocence I'd assumed that the magnificent Cally would still be where it had always been, and I'd walked along the main street of Tamworth looking for it. But Peel Street seemed to be wall-to-wall unlovely chain stores: Kmart, Sportsgirl, Darrell Lea, the gaudy face of commerce. When I reached the end of the shops I turned around and went back down the other side of the street, in case a two-storey hotel as big as an ocean liner had somehow tucked itself away between Rebel Sports and Soul Pattinson.

I stopped one or two people to ask. *I'm looking for the Caledonian Hotel. Could you put me right for the Caledonian Hotel?* I went for older ones who looked like long-time locals, and they were friendly, they didn't do that flinch-and-frozen-face thing that city people do when a stranger approaches them on the street. But no one could tell me where it was.

Finally I tried at the post office, one of the few dignified old buildings that had escaped the wrecking. It was a silly impulse, that an old building would have in it someone who knew about another old building, but I wasn't giving up without a fight. I bought a book of stamps and asked the pleasant woman serving me. She was surprised, but understood with one glance that I was looking for family history.

Oh yes, she said. I'm sorry, love, it was pulled down years ago.

Where was it? I asked.

I had a silly sense that if could stand on the spot there'd be … something, a vibration of the past coming up through the ground.

She broke it to me as gently as she could. Well, love, she said, it was where Kmart is.

She looked away, fiddled with some papers.

Actually … it was where the Kmart parking lot is.

She couldn't look me in the face.

Go to Kmart, she said finally, briskly. Stand in the parking lot behind it. That's where the Cally was.

The Kmart parking lot! Back in 2012 I didn't think I needed to subject myself to that. Better to hang onto my image of the grand Cally and my mother's pride in it.

But now, out of some sense of a job not finished, of having taken a shortcut to avoid something I wasn't going to like, I'm doing as she said. Past the bulky mass of Kmart, through a narrow alleyway, and here it is, the parking lot where the grand Caledonian once was. A man with his keys out, walking towards his ute with the dog tied up in the tray, stares at me under his hat, this woman standing as if lost in the middle of the Kmart car park. Cars glinting in the sun, the heat beating up from the bitumen, and people with trolleys pushing all the junk they've just bought.

It's the glare, I suppose. The sun in my eyes. And I'm probably dehydrated. I shouldn't be this upset about the fact that the Caledonian is gone.

I wonder what was in the minds of the Tamworth city fathers when they decided to swing the wrecking ball at their own past. They weren't alone. I remember the Sydney of my young days as a place in the grip of an ecstasy of demolition. The magnificent old Queen Victoria Building was only saved because at the eleventh hour a Malaysian company saw a way for it to turn a profit.

Standing there in the car park, with not a single old thing in sight, I think I understand what the demolition is about. Deep down we knew we'd done wrong in taking the place the way we did. That left a shadow no one wanted to look at, and the old buildings held the shadow. Getting rid of the buildings was a way of getting rid of the shadow.

The other thing I did on that earlier trip was go to the family history centre.

I've never been too keen on these family history places – never wanted to be another of those bright-eyed women putting every last twig on the family tree. It felt self-absorbed, even narcissistic, and too many of those bright-eyed women were hoping to find a long-lost duke in the family. Still, I was there in Tamworth, and the thing I was hoping to find was well and truly gone. So much had been lost – was there something I could salvage? I was a bit shamefaced about it, but I headed towards the centre on Napier Street.

It was a couple of upstairs rooms full of wooden filing cabinets and big heavy tables for people to spread out their papers. I could see the place was immaculately organised, filing cabinets and card files, books all with their Dewey numbers on the spine. A young

Queen smiled serenely out from the wall and below her an ornate antique globe of the world was mostly pink.

Women bustled about, bending over papers and turning from one shelf and filing cabinet to another. In one corner in important solitude an old gentleman in tweed looked through a thick book, his fountain pen poised to write in the notebook beside him.

The volunteers were obliging, and the friendly woman who appointed herself my guide through the filing system was courteously interested in why I was doing family history. Like the other volunteers, she was nicely dressed and nicely spoken, and I guessed that family history was an interest because her own family was well established. Of course I was making assumptions, but I was picturing her family tree as being innocent of convicts or other taints.

Now, where was your grandfather's property? she asked. There were some Russells out Manilla way – they had one of the biggest runs in the area. Beautiful homestead, on the National Trust Register. He was a member of parliament, I think, or was it a judge?

No, he owned the Caledonian, I said.

The Caledonian ... it rings a bell ...

It was a hotel, I explained. A pub.

Oh, a pub!

How horrified she'd probably be if I told her something else I knew about my grandfather. One day Mum had thought to send away for his birth certificate. I remember her coming to me with the certificate in her hand and a strange look on her face. She held it out so I could see the word *ILLEGITIMATE* scrawled across the page, corner to corner.

Many people who find something like that in their family tree do their best to hide it, but the funny look on Mum's face wasn't shame. It was disappointment. She'd wanted to find out more about her father and, beyond him, her grandfather on that side. I'd like to know too. But the blank in the column for *father's name* means that we can't. That particular branch of our family tree will always be missing.

The volunteer showed me how the place worked. You started off with one of the index-card files, then that cross-referenced to a big black binder that cross-referenced in turn to a filing cabinet with its own sub-index that led to Drawer Three. Drawer Three contained thick plastic binders in alphabetical order. One of them was labelled *Hotels*, and it had a list of the owners of the Cally, starting with Mrs Trim back in the 1870s.

But there was no sign of Albert Russell, let alone his wife, Dolly. I went back to the pleasant lady, gave her the dates again, and we went through the routine once more: index cards, big black binder, filing cabinet, Drawer Three, Hotels folder. She was becoming a little flustered, turning through the folder backwards and forwards.

Russell, you said?

I'd been conscious of another woman, higher up the ranks here in the family history centre. She'd been keeping an eye on us, and now she could see there was a little *moment* happening here under the antique globe. She moved over to us and the friendly volunteer explained.

This second woman was the head prefect type. She looked as though she was experienced at dealing with little *moments* that popped up, and knew how to squash them.

Yes, I see, she said. We can make some enquiries. In the meantime, you might find something in this.

She reached smoothly to the bookcase and took down a book

about Tamworth. A large-format book, lots of photos, glossy paper. She pulled out a chair, opened the book, showed me the table of contents.

Have a look here, I would, she said. See if you can find anything.

I wasn't interested in a book. I could have seen that in the library in Sydney. Still, I noticed the author's name, a writer of excellent, well-researched books, including a detailed account of the Myall Creek massacre. This would be more than a coffee-table book. There was no point making any more fuss about Albert Russell's absence from the file. I did as she was almost physically pushing me to do. I sat down and opened the book.

There were Russells in the index, but none of them was mine. And the Caledonian didn't get a mention. If it hadn't been for the woman in the post office, by this stage I'd have been thinking that Mum must have gone off into an imaginary Tamworth that never existed.

I was glancing through the chapter about the years my family was here, and there was a photo of the Tamworth High School hockey team of 1928, a row of smiling girls. The photo was a bit crooked with excitement because they'd just won the pennant two of them were holding out between them. And there was Mum! Unmistakably my sixteen-year-old mother, beaming away with the others.

Oh, I exclaimed, a bit too loudly for this quiet room and these polite ladies. There's my mother!

I ran my finger along the names. *Name*, *name*, *name*, but where my mother's name should have been, *unknown*.

I can put this right, I said. This is my mother, Nance Russell.

My pen was poised to add my mother's name to the 1928 hockey team, but the head woman made a noise of ladylike protest that was almost a scream.

Oh no, she cried, we mustn't write in the book!

There was a stiff silence in the room. Even the man in tweed glanced up. Then everyone went back to rustling their papers and turning their pages.

As I left – to make mischief, really, because I was pretty sure I already knew the answer – I asked if there was anything about Aboriginal families among the papers here.

Oh, not really, Head Prefect said. Her voice had gone a bit thin. There weren't many Aboriginal people in town until recently.

That was her closing the door, but like a persistent salesperson I stuck my foot in it.

Ah, I said innocently, and where were they?

Oh well, she said, they were in the housing commission and so on.

Which I supposed was one kind of answer to the question, *Where were the Aboriginal people?*

Even back in 2012 I had a fair idea why Aboriginal family history wouldn't have had much of a look-in at the family history centre, but I know a good bit more now. In the years my family was in Tamworth, Aboriginal people were everywhere. Some were out on those reserves or missions. Others were still living in pastoral camps on sheep or cattle stations out in the country. Some were in camps on the outskirts of towns, living and working on the edge of the white world. Quite a few were moving around as itinerant workers on farms, or following the fruit on orchards.

But wherever they were, they were keeping a low profile, because they lived in daily fear of their children being taken from them. The efforts to *breed out the colour* had become even more vigorous, and from 1915, the Aborigines Protection Board had the legal right to remove children from their families. They no longer had to claim that the children were orphaned or neglected. Thousands of children – many only babies – were forcibly taken from their families and put in those institutions, *boarding schools* or *training homes*, that had been set up with the specific intention of separating them from their families. In those bleak places they never saw their families or learned anything about them. Many were told their parents were dead. Others were told, even more cruelly, that their parents had chosen to send them away. At the end of their *apprenticeship* the children were sent to work for white families as labourers or domestic servants.

There are many firsthand accounts of how Aboriginal people evaded being *bred out*. Families kept moving, to stay a step ahead of the officials. Their children were blackened with charcoal to make them less light-skinned. Children were taught to run and hide if they saw any white men. No wonder there *weren't many Aboriginal people in town till recently*. Pragmatic and strategic as ever, they'd made themselves and their children as invisible as possible.

My grandparents must have known about children being removed. It wasn't a secret. They would have been told all the pretexts about it being *for their own good*, and how it would *give the little half-castes the opportunity to better themselves*. But did they believe them?

This generation of the family stories is the first within my own memory – I knew Dolly and Bert, though not well enough to be sure how they felt about their government's actions. But I'm trying now to put my knowledge of them in the same frame as my knowledge of what was going on around them.

I remember my grandmother as a stern, disapproving, cranky old woman. I could imagine her being judgemental and unsympathetic towards Aboriginal people. She might have swallowed the idea that the best thing to be was white, and the quicker the black people became white, the better for everyone. On the other hand, as a woman of that time, she knew what it was like to be excluded and belittled, regarded as second-class, and to possess no real power. Some women accepted that as their destiny, but she chafed against the limitations of her life. That might have given her some understanding.

I remember my grandfather, too – in his last years he came to live with us. He'd been a shearer and a farmer, and he would have stayed on the farm all his life except that Dolly had banged the saucepan on the stove and insisted that they leave. When I knew Grandpa, he was an old man with a whistling hearing aid who shaved with a frightening straight-edge razor that he sharpened on a leather strop hanging from the bathroom washbasin. He'd kept the *blades* he'd used in his shearing days, oiled and wrapped up in a worn-out singlet.

He'd grown up on the wrong side of the tracks. His mother called herself a widow but she was always pregnant. In the Russell house, a day when you had a scrape of dripping to put on your bread was a day better than most. Grandpa would have worked alongside Aboriginal men in his shearing and rouseabout days, and he might have judged another man on what sort of person he was rather than on the colour of his skin.

I'd like to think that both my grandparents might have had their hearts in the right place. I can even make a case for it, based on what I know of their own lives. But whatever they really thought, and whatever I like to hope, they were part of a world that allowed terrible things to be done.

Recently I came across some astonishing information about the ways many First Nations languages embed family or kinship structures in their grammar. The word you use in referring to someone – *him* or *her* – can be modified so it carries information about what relation that person is to the speaker, and to the person being spoken to. If I'm getting even a superficial understanding of what I've read, that means a person might say, *I gave it to him*, and the exact form of the words would convey not just the fact of something being given, but also the family relationships between the speaker, the hearer, and the person being referred to.

These are cultures where kinship links are so strong and so vital to the meaning of the universe that they're woven into the very warp and weft of the language. That gives a whole appalling extra dimension to the cruelty of taking children away. What kind of existential chaos must ensue when those links are broken?

Try as they might, the balanda didn't succeed in erasing the First Nations. But all those children taken from their families meant that several generations of children all over Australia, in numbers that are contested but certainly enormous, grew up not knowing anything about where they came from or who they were. There were no family history centres for them.

There's another side to it, though. When Mum came to me with her father's birth certificate and the look of loss on her face, it meant the end of the road. We will never know anything about that side of the family. But when the ripping-up of families was inflicted on the First Nations, the road didn't always end there.

I've many times heard one Aboriginal person ask another, Where's your mob from? There'll be a long convoluted conversation about great-aunts and great-great-uncles and great-aunts of second cousins twice removed. Eventually they'll find how their mobs are connected. Then they'll get on with the conversation.

That's how the intricate webs of family connections were often kept alive, carried along through generations of oral stories and all those remembered links to the great-aunts of second cousins twice removed. In some cases, enough knowledge survived for families to knit themselves up again later. The records they had – nothing more than stories carried from one voice to another – seemed fragile. But sometimes they turned out to be stronger than any official piece of paper.

The Aboriginal writer Melissa Lucashenko floored me when I met her for the first time in 2001. She asked me that same question: Where's your mob from? It sounded a simple enough question but I didn't seem to know how to answer it. What I stammered out to her was based on the family stories, that feeble string of beads handed on from mother to daughter as if they were precious. Solomon Wiseman was from London – does that mean I'm *from* London? Or *from* Cork in Ireland, where they say *chainies*? Or North Sydney, where that whale-on-the-rock engraved itself into my memory? There were too many *froms*. In any case, Melissa wasn't asking about geography. I think now that she was challenging me to think about what it means to be descended from the colonists.

Melissa's question – and the sad muddle of my answer – is in many ways where all the thinking and writing I've done since then has sprung from. A person who can't answer that question surely has a blank space in their sense of themselves and their *mob* – a blank that needs to be thought about. Where *is* my mob from?

That's the question lying behind all those family history centres. What that whole genealogy industry is really doing is trying to establish a provenance for ourselves. It's what you'd do if you'd just bought a painting by a famous artist and you wanted to make sure it was the real thing: you'd go backwards from the person who owns it now, and identify every previous owner, one by one, right back to the artist. If you can establish that unbroken chain of ownership, you know the painting isn't a forgery. So we name all the names in an unbroken line – father to son, mother to daughter – and place ourselves there on the line. We're trying to authenticate ourselves.

But listen to my scorn about having an interest in family history! Of course – I'm scornful because I'm part of it, with my scribbled family trees and my slips of family history. It's true that an interest in one's forebears can get distorted into snobbery, and the authenticating impulse can be a kind of denial. But at the same time, we balandas need to be asking questions about our forebears.

Not to reassure ourselves, and not to make any claims for ourselves, but to learn how we really fit – and the ways we don't fit – into the story of being here.

I've tried to find out more about Dad's family too, but Dad only ever had one story about his forebears, and there was always a whiff of the fanciful about it. He'd had it from his mother, he said. She'd told him that her great-great-whatever was Sir Richard Grenville, cousin of Sir Walter Raleigh, hero of the Armada. Tennyson wrote a poem about him, of which Dad would often declaim the first line. "At Flores, in the Azores, Sir Richard Grenville lay." He only knew one other bit and he'd hastily skip to that: "Fall into the hands of God, not into the hands of Spain!"

There was always something self-mocking about Dad's declaiming of those scraps and I was never sure why. Was it that, as a Trotskyite revolutionary (ret'd), he had no time for the aristocracy or poems about their valour? Or was it that he was proud – not everyone has an ancestor featured in a Tennyson poem, after all – but embarrassed to be proud? Or did he only half-believe the story?

I'm ashamed to say that I also occasionally boasted about Sir Richard Grenville, and declaimed the same two lines. I was self-mocking, too. Like Dad, I was having it both ways – laughing at having such an illustrious ancestor, but proud of it too.

So when a relative on the Grenville side got in touch and told me the Sir Richard Grenville story was nonsense, I was pleased to have it cleared up. This distant cousin told me that our original Grenville forebear, George, had been given as a baby to the Foundling Hospital in London in about 1764.

The Foundling Hospital was set up as an act of charity by a seaman-made-good, to give a home to some of the thousands of *illegitimate* children in London. There were a lot of them because, beyond the genteel world of Jane Austen novels, and in the absence of contraception, a lot of babies were conceived, as the old phrase went, out of wedlock. The future, for the babies and the *fallen women* who were their mothers, was extremely bleak.

The idea that beneficent seaman had was that, if there was somewhere to put the baby, the mother might have a chance to start again. The sentimental fiction was that she might find a husband and could then come back and reclaim the child. To make that possible, the mother left a "token" with the child – a piece of fabric, half a playing card, a button.

But in the meantime, the child's identity had to be hidden behind a new name, so the mother could make that fresh start. From lack of imagination, or maybe as a cruel joke, the clerks often gave the poor little scraps of life grand names: Caesar, Hannibal, Samson. Other babies were given the names of poets or politicians. When my forebear arrived at the Foundling Hospital, the prime minister happened to be an incompetent fellow by the name of George Grenville.

So much for *Flores in the Azores.*

In 2001 I was in London, and with some time on my hands I went to the Foundling Hospital, a lovely old building in Bloomsbury, and then to the London Metropolitan Archives, to see if I could find my George Grenville. At the archives, the cranky woman behind the counter was finally persuaded to entrust me with a ledger fattened by the sad little tokens attached to each page. George Grenville had a faded square of cheap blue gingham. No one had ever come for him.

I cheered that sailor for his kindness. He probably saved my forebear from an early death. Still, it made for a bit of a blank. The efficiency of the Foundling Hospital in hiding the real names of the babies meant that a few generations later, a person looking for their forebear couldn't even guess at who or what came before George Grenville, transported to Australia in 1836. Even George Grenville wouldn't have known.

He'd have known that he wasn't the son of the prime minister and wasn't descended from Sir Richard Grenville. But he, or his son or grandson, decided to start that story. It was a reinvention of self that was one of the many perks of transportation, the ultimate fresh start. After all, once you've got nowhere to put your feet in a new place, you have to invent the ground to stand on. While you're at it, you might as well invent the feet as well.

I turned the pages of the register, thinking of the hopeless pain of those poor women, so carefully cutting the playing card in half, choosing a button she had two of, and my own particular, forever unknown great-great-great-grandmother, snipping the square of blue gingham from the corner of her apron, planning how she would return – any day now! – and hold up the apron to show the official the missing square and be given her baby back.

That's terribly sad. But sitting there in London, on the other side of the world from home, the thing that was rising into my throat was the thought of all those babies stolen from their mothers, back where I live. There were no tokens for them, no sentimental fictions about being reunited, nothing but the cruel pseudoscience of *breeding out the colour*.

I'd always been appalled by what we did. But it had been an abstract thing. There'd been no scrap of cheap blue gingham to make it real. Holding the ugly bulging register in that airless London archive room, the librarian watching me suspiciously, I felt a kind of vomit of disgust, not for the sadness I was holding in my hand, but for the one I'd left, back home.

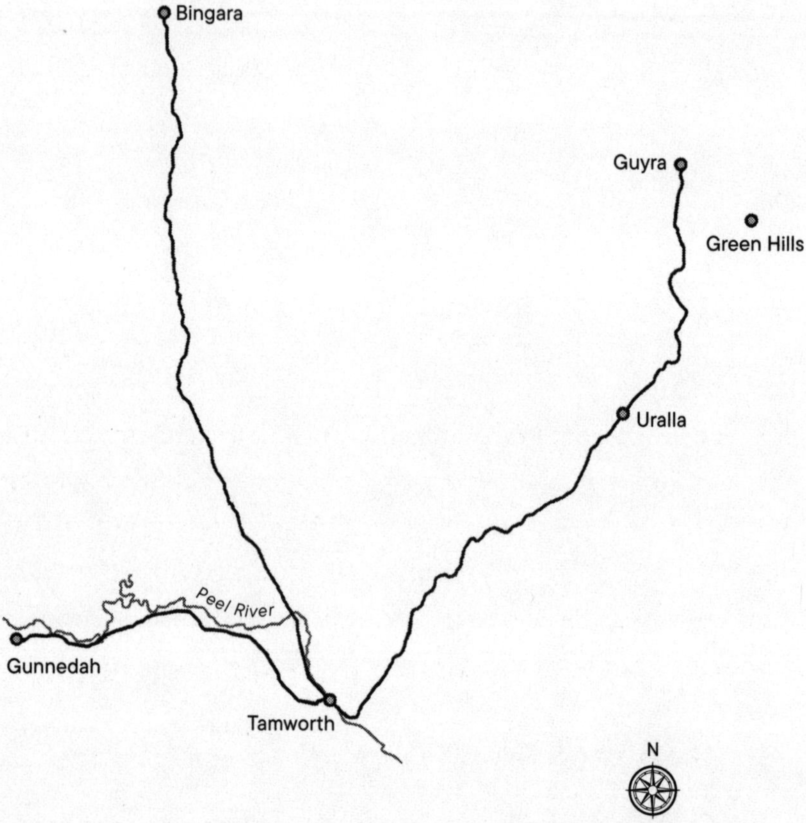
Bingara
Guyra
Green Hills
Uralla
Peel River
Gunnedah
Tamworth
N
0
30
Kilometres

URALLA

The next bit of family story is at Guyra, but on the way there's no avoiding the bushranger Thunderbolt. He's the big thing for tourists at Uralla, halfway between Tamworth and Guyra. I'm not interested in Thunderbolt, and there's no family story about him, but the family does have a connection to him, because he held up John Davis's hotel at Currabubula.

> Dec 16, 1865, Maitland Mercury
>
> On Dec 9, 1865, Thunderbolt and two of his mates, armed and each leading a pack horse, stuck up Mr John Martin Davis's inn at Currabubula. They took eighteen pounds in notes and cheques from a box belonging to Mr Davis's son and a new saddle. They called for bottled porter, which they paid for, and then left. One of them was riding the racehorse Eucalyptus.

That must have been a memorable day, so it's surprising that Thunderbolt doesn't get a mention in the family stories. Possibly the people who had dealings with him didn't find him as romantic as the tourists do these days. Eighteen pounds was a lot of money and there'd have been no insurance to buy yourself a new saddle.

The nom-de-guerre *Captain Thunderbolt* conjures up visions of an aristocrat-turned-bushranger with some kind of tragic opera-plot past, but Captain Thunderbolt was actually plain Fred Ward, a working-class boy from Windsor who stole some horses, spent some time in the slammer, escaped, and took up bushranging.

Around Uralla he's a big tourist attraction. The Captain Thunderbolt Sites are on the State Heritage Register. There's his Rock, his Cave, his Death Site and his Grave.

Thunderbolt's Rock is on a piece of high ground right beside the highway. It's a startling piece of topography, so I pull into the lay-by. It's actually not one rock but a cluster of them, huge weathered masses of granite standing at the top of a grassy hill. They lean and huddle together like a crowd of big round people. The humanoid shape of the rocks gives them a powerful attraction. Everyone stops, the way I've just done, and takes a photo.

The balanda story about these rocks is that Captain Thunderbolt and his men would hide behind them and pop out to hold up the coaches at gunpoint. Strip everyone of their cash and watches and jewellery, ride off into the sunset. But there'd always have been stories about this spectacular landmark, I think, long before Thunderbolt came along.

I don't carry any kind of torch for Thunderbolt, but I'm shocked at what we've done to his Rock – it's covered with graffiti. HMA, KT, LEONA KANE, a weathered blur above and below a huge red LOVES. These marks aren't the impulse of a moment – get out the penknife and carve your initials into the bark of a tree. You've planned it. It seems like a fun thing to do. You've bought paint, you've thought about what colour you want. You've got the brush, and you've remembered to bring along a screwdriver to open the tin, and something to stir the paint with so it sticks properly. You've come all the way out here in your car, probably with a mate. You'd have got up very early to do it when no one was around, or very late at night. You drop the tin of paint, the brush, the screwdriver, the stirring-stick over the fence and then climb through and get to work. What a lark.

You stand back when you're done, but somehow putting your initials over everything hasn't given the satisfaction you'd hoped for. You come in with the brush and the tin of paint and you do it again, bigger, on another part of the rock. In the end – you can see where someone's done it – you take the tin in both hands and splash a great dollop of it over the rock and watch it drip thickly down into the grass.

You'd have been laughing, but there's no getting away from the fact that there's something angry happening here. There's a cutting-something-down-to-size. The peculiar huddling and embracing rocks, and their strange isolation in the landscape, make them things of enormous beauty and force. They come from another mode, another logic, another way of being. They say something about time beyond human understanding, the patient time of the planet where rocks erupt and take a million years to be weathered, molecule by molecule, into these fantastical smooth sculptural shapes.

If you come from a culture that doesn't know how to accommodate that kind of time, it could make you feel small. If you come from the kind of culture that thinks the self is the centre of the world, you might hear these rocks telling you you're wrong, that you don't even register on the kind of timeframe these ancient forms come from. That mightn't be something you want to hear.

What people have done to the Rock has set me thinking about what it means to want to force yourself on something, the way those people have forced themselves on those rocks, so I'm interested enough to stop when I see a sign for Thunderbolt's Cave. It's a short walk through lovely muted stringybark bush, on a steep slope where the loose stones would make it hard for anyone to creep up unheard. The cave is a jagged hole in a hillside of rough dark rock. It faces south so it's sunless and glum. It's not enticing. I have to make myself go in. A low entrance opens into a dome-roofed space about the size of a small bedroom. I suppose a few people could live there, though you'd like it better if you weren't too tall. There's a sort of back entrance which would be handy as a chimney or an escape route. People have left their mark here too: scraps of toilet paper and a crude charcoal scrawl of a cock and balls.

It would be hard to find unless you knew where it was, so it was a good hiding place. But this is the reality behind the romantic legend: crouching here with your offsiders on these rough rocks, hunched over the tiny fire that was all you could safely light, hitting your head on the roof if you stood up too quickly, in this dank claustrophobic place whose only merit was that the troopers were unlikely to find you.

Ward was finally caught and shot beside a stream in a paddock not far away. The stream was later dammed so the actual Death Site is now somewhere under the water. However, apparently the paddock is heritage-listed.

I have a good laugh over the idea of a heritage-listed paddock, but there's something I find revolting about this fetishisation of Fred Ward and the others like him. *Bushranger*. What an aura of larrikin glamour the word conjures up. It's something about the idea of *ranging*. There's a suggestion of freedom, of being out on the range, ranging freely.

Those men – Thunderbolt, Ned Kelly, Ben Hall – they're all romantic legends, what chambers of commerce like to call *Australian icons*. In fact they were violent criminals. Ward held up mail coaches, pubs and private homes at gunpoint and robbed rich and poor alike. His gun wasn't just for show. He shot – or certainly shot at – at least three policemen.

But I suppose you don't have to dig very deep to work out why we love them. It makes us feel good to glamorise those thieves, because thieves are what we are too.

The most interesting thing to me about the Thunderbolt story is what it often leaves out: his wife, Mary Ann Bugg. Mary Ann helped him escape from Cockatoo Island jail (the legend is that she swam across shark-infested waters with a file between her teeth), hid him from the police, brought him supplies when he was in hiding, and even showed him where those hiding places were. She might have showed him the cave I saw. She's not part of the Boys' Own adventure story, but he couldn't have done it without her. That deserves honouring, in a world that still puts men at the centre.

But the other significant thing about her is that she was an Aboriginal woman. She's been erased twice, you might say – once as a woman and again as an Aboriginal person.

There's a studio photo of Mary Ann Bugg, a woman in conventional late-Victorian dress: enormous skirt, narrow waist, puffed sleeves. She's posed with one hand on the back of an elaborate barley-twist chair and there's a suggestion of draped curtains behind her. Along the bottom, in a big clear hand that can't be ignored or mistaken, is the title: "Thunderbolt's Gin".

This photo isn't part of most of the tourist bumph you see about Captain Thunderbolt. Where it is displayed, the label has usually been cut off the bottom of the image. Which I understand – these days no one wants to see something so offensive. But maybe we should. Maybe we shouldn't pick and choose among the relics of the past and only display the ones that don't make us uncomfortable. Behind that offensive label lies the past that belongs to us balanda, like it or not. That photo, with its label, should be displayed right up there with the portrait of Fred Ward. The signage should acknowledge what we were, and apologise for it. Not to be too pious, but we should take responsibility for the ugly parts of our heritage, along with the prettier bits.

GUYRA

The Cally was lost to our family long before it was demolished. My grandparents took on a huge debt to buy it in 1927. Then the Depression came and in 1931 they defaulted on the mortgage. Mum was in Sydney, working as a pharmacist, but the rest of the family spent the next few years eking out an existence on the only thing they could salvage, a scratchy little farm near Mittagong. Then Frank, Mum's older brother, managed to find a way out.

> Frank used to go in for these ballots, they'd ballot the land. He came to me and he said, Can you lend me fifty pounds? I need fifty pounds to put in it. So I lent him that. The fifty pounds was just to show you were bona fide. If you hadn't won, you would have got your money back, I think.

> I had to go and get it out of my passbook. He paid me back terribly quickly. I would have wanted it back, I wasn't giving it to him. That was about all I had in the bank.
>
> It was around the time the Depression was ending – around 1938, I think. Frank won a block of land near Guyra. He and Dad left Mittagong and went up there.

That farm – Green Hills – is the last stop on this journey, the last generation before mine. The last generation of what you might call *settlers*, before it all got unsettled.

North of Tamworth there's a broad, open valley. Then the road heads straight at an imposing range of steep high hills and within a few minutes it's noticeably cooler and the whole face of the country is completely different. This area is now called New England, so someone must have thought it was like England, but it's not like any part of it that I've ever seen. Homesickness can be a distorting window for framing a landscape.

This is a place of wild gullies and peaks, of grey granite lumps pushing up through the ground, of huge rounded tors piled on each other. When the road curves to let you see into the distance, it's all rearing heaps of bush-covered hills, their steep slopes leaning the same way like cows in a paddock, with glimpses of the great speckled plain that I'm climbing out of. There's a sense of vastness, boundarylessness, a place that's endlessly and scarily wild.

As the road takes me further and further, grinding up the steep pinches of the Moonbi Range, I realise how pleased I am to have left the valley of the Peel behind. It was full of houses and roads and neat paddocks of green, and I seem to want to be out among something wilder. I'm trying to go backwards in time, and all those neat paddocks obscure the past.

Then the land opens out again. I'm going along the plateau at the top of the range. It's bare, windswept, even bleak. There are big paddocks of rough, tufty grass and heaps of rocks piled here and there as if someone's tried to clear them. Up here it's mostly sheep country. The sheep look like the rounded weathered granite: the same grey, the same rounded lump. You have to look twice to see if it's a rock or a sheep.

As I get close to Guyra the highway takes another step upwards. I can see we're going through a kind of pass between mountains. Guyra must be on the next level of the plateau. The trees here are quite different – not the smooth gumtrees I saw lower down. These are all very rough, stringybark or ironbark, I don't know my eucalypts, only that these sombre stands of light-absorbing bark make the place solemn and somehow watchful.

I pass a sign: *Poison Swamp Creek.* Now that I've started thinking about names, there's no escaping them.

Guyra is 60 ks north of Uralla and some 450 ks from Sydney. It's like a set designer's idea of a small quiet country town. The story would be about a talented boy or girl, desperate to get out into the world of art they were destined for, and the gravitational pull of the town, how hard it would be to catapult yourself out of it. The happy ending would be a shot of the town shrinking in the distance out the back window of the bus.

The town is to one side of the highway. There's a short main street with modest shopfronts of a 1920s vintage. An old labrador saunters across the road, ignoring a huge truck bearing down on it. I don't think you have to hurry very often in Guyra. Today everything seems to be closed.

Funny, all at once I'm feeling a strange kind of panic here. Guyra is more or less like all the other small towns I've been through on the trip, but I thought they were rather attractive. Here I feel only that I want to leave.

I turn into a side street and see one more shop, in among houses. It's got a big sign on the awning: *Bookshop Plumber*, and in the window I can see it's got books on one side and pipes on the other. Well, why not, husband and wife, she's always wanted to have a second-hand bookshop ... from the sign alone a certain kind of whimsical novel just about writes itself.

The town is where it is because of a place with the wonderful name of Mother of Ducks Lagoon. It's a big body of water surrounded by a wetland that teems with what the tourist sign calls *wildlife*, but which two hundred years ago would more likely have been thought of as *food*. Not only ducks, but dozens of other kinds of birds, plus yabbies and eels and, of course, fish. Gara is said to mean *fish may be caught* in the local language. As I read that on the National Parks sign, I think it's an oddly prim way of putting it. And oddly ambiguous. Does it mean *if you're lucky you'll catch a fish*, or *you're allowed to catch fish*?

The lagoon is now a sanctuary with a birdwatching platform and pictures of the many kinds of birds that come here to fill up before making one of their epic flights. I can see a huge flock of something, though I can't identify it from the pictures. It's exhilarating, seeing them wheel and swoop and come to land beside a patch of reeds.

The lagoon is now much smaller than it used to be. When the balanda first came here they grazed their cattle beside it, and then after a while they set about "reclaiming" parts of it to increase the land for their stock. And what a peculiar word that is to describe what they did. *Reclaim* is what you do when you take back something that belongs to you. It's as if the place was always supposed to be a cow paddock and the water covering it was some kind of mistake. Reclaiming it was fixing the mistake.

They kept some of the lagoon and it became famous as a place for "shootists" to hunt birds for sport. But as time went on, more was reclaimed for a showground, a racecourse and a golf course. Mother of Ducks became Mother of Golf Balls.

Times change, priorities change, and some of what was *reclaimed* has now been *re-reclaimed* and allowed to become wetland again. The birds have come back, and probably you *may*, or *can*, catch fish once more in the stream that flows past the birdwatching platform.

It's said that the *explorer* John Oxley was the first foreigner to see this part of the world, though he mightn't have come this far north. In any case, by the 1830s the squatters had moved in. In the words of a local history, Alexander Campbell *took up* a stretch of land he called Guyra Station in 1835. In 1838 the Everett brothers *founded*

Ollera Station to the west, and others *settled* to the east along the Gara River, on a big area the squatter called Green Hills. At that stage it was described as *practically virgin land.* Hmmm. Can you be practically a virgin? That *practically* doesn't intend to, but it points to the fact that the land was being used and manipulated by Aboriginal people in ways that even the balanda could see.

At some point that big run called Green Hills became a pastoral lease. The lease changed hands a few times before being sold to the government in 1936 – which was a bit of right-hand-not-knowing-what-the-left-was-doing, since it was a lease and in theory the government already owned it. The government subdivided it into fourteen smaller blocks that were balloted to be sold.

This balloting was one more flange on the massive superstructure of legality that sat on top of the original theft initiated by Captain Cook. It was the latest in the government's efforts to break up the enormous squatting runs. There'd been *Selection*. Then, after World War One, there'd been the *Soldier Settler Scheme*. Now Frank was benefitting from the *Closer Settlement Scheme*. When I'd skimmed over that phrase in my reading I'd vaguely thought it meant settlement closer to the cities, but what the government had in mind was *denser* settlement.

All these ways of carving the place up were partly about reducing the power of the squatters. But the other reason seems to have been the deep-rooted cultural memory of a European landscape, a picture of what countryside ought to look like. The idea was that Australia's future would be as a country of yeoman farmers working tame, tidy farms on a human scale.

The balloting business was to make it fair, or at least look fair. You had to put down a deposit – that must have been the fifty pounds Frank borrowed from Mum. If you won the block, you took out a mortgage with the Rural Bank and were supposed to do the same sort of *improvements* as the selectors had had to do.

There were forty-six applicants for the Guyra ballot, but the Land Board eliminated eighteen of them. It had learned from earlier schemes that if people didn't have experience of farming it would be tears before bedtime. Frank – with a few years on his uncle's farm behind him – was one of twenty-eight remaining applicants for the fourteen blocks.

I'm glad he won the block. From all accounts he was a good fellow and his own farm was what he'd longed for. But good fellow and all that he was – my mother's favourite brother, the victim of a war that had nothing to do with him – the fact is that Uncle Frank was just one more in the string of balanda who'd taken that land. The "fair" method of balloting it was really nothing more than a re-run of what had always happened everywhere on the continent: the Crown had taken the land and given it away to whomever they wanted to.

Did Frank ever think about the people whose land he was on? Who knows, but probably not, or not much. Between the first settler in the 1830s and Frank in 1938, there'd have been half-a-dozen different owners. A hundred years would have passed since Aboriginal people had lived there in their traditional ways without disruption. Easy for Frank to put them out of mind, as they might have been out of sight.

Still, I was interested to read that in the 2021 census, nearly 10 per cent of people in this area identified as Aboriginal. That's more than double the national average. Now that's what you call survival.

Frank won the ballot in 1938. A year later, World War Two started.

> When the war started, he joined up. He volunteered.
> He just chose the wrong moment, joined the 8th Division.
> Dad said to him, I'll look after the farm, do my very best
> till you come back.
>
> Frank went to the war and didn't come back. That's how Dad got Guyra. It was Frank's property. Dad deserved it because he worked hard and put all he could into it. If Frank had come back, it would have been to a good property.

For his whole life, Frank had wanted nothing more than to be a farmer with land of his own. He'd only had Green Hills for a year before the war started. He enlisted, he was sent to fight in Timor and he became a prisoner of the Japanese. He died on the Burma Railway and never saw Green Hills again. For my mother, grief about her brother's pointless death was a wound in her psyche that never healed.

Every place I've been through on this trip – even the smallest village that's nothing more than a service station and a skew-whiff shed – has a war memorial. Mostly it takes the form of a column with the names of faraway places carved into marble or granite and picked out in gold leaf, and the names of the local boys who died there lined up in alphabetical order, as the boys themselves must have lined up to go into class at school. There's usually a statue as well. The soldier on the plinth is often the same one from town to town, a job lot for the local monument-maker. He's a young man staring blandly off into the distance, his digger's hat shading his face, his rifle upright at his side, his puttees like bandages around his calves.

A lot of places also have a gun, sometimes a massive World War One cannon but more often a smaller one on wheels from World War Two. Uncle Frank was a bombardier. He'd have used one of those. You'd think they'd have wanted to leave them behind when the war finished, never think about them again. But they put them on a boat and brought them back! Perhaps they'd developed a kind of affection for the weapons that had come to feel like friends, defending them from the people who were trying to kill them.

Guyra doesn't just have a stained white statue but also a small building with *Soldiers Memorial Hall* over the door. It's been made with great care, like any other temple, with some masterly brickwork in contrasting liver and sand colours. The bronze honour roll from World War Two is up there with the one for the Glorious Dead from the Great War and the Boer War. So many young men from this one country area. All those lives snuffed out, all those futures turned into a bit of dust in some foreign place.

The only other time I've been here in Guyra was the day twenty years ago when the World War Two honour roll was unveiled. The man who was organising the refurbishment of the memorial had somehow tracked my brother down and invited him to the unveiling of the new plaque on Anzac Day.

My brother wasn't planning to go, but I decided to be there. Partly it was for Frank. He died before I was born, but I had an impulse to greet him across the years, to honour the sad story of a lost life. More than that, it was because Mum had died not long before, and this felt like a chance to connect to a part of her life that had been so significant to her.

Not that she'd have wanted to be there. The whole subject of Anzac Day was always a no-go area at home. Mum hated the day and all its grand sentiments. She'd much rather have had her brother than a lot of hot air about valour and honour. She had nothing but bitter feelings for the war, for the men who'd sent her brother to fight, for the British who'd taken so many of our soldiers and left so few to defend our own country.

Bitter, too, about all the hoopla on the day. She felt there was a quality of gloating about it. Yes, we'll march and look solemn but then it's a booze-up with our mates. We're alive and they're dead. *Lest We Forget*, everyone mouths. *Lest We Forget*, up in gold on a thousand memorials.

I'd absorbed her resistance, and every time I see those words I wonder again at them. Put in plain English, we're saying, *In case we forget*. In other words, we're saying we might.

Today, standing in the wind outside the Memorial Hall, watching the flag ripple at the top of its pole – the stars that are ours, and the Union Jack that belongs to someone else – I'm inclined to feel my mother's revulsion at the whole thing, but when I was here all those years ago I was pleased to be part of it. I'd driven to Guyra, spent the night in the motel, set the alarm for the Dawn Service, and gone out into the frosty morning to join the small crowd on the main street.

There was a man with a bugle doing the Last Post. There was a lot of ceremony with the flag – unfolding it, holding it out to be hoisted, and a nasty moment when it wouldn't rise because the rope kept getting twisted back on itself. Finally a man stepped forward and did something quietly forceful to it and the flag jerked up to the top of the pole. There was the solemn bit of Kipling and some prayers and a short speech by a man in a suit. It was very cold, that damp, dank cold that gets through any number of layers. I stood there at one side of the crowd, too numb with the cold and the early hour to feel anything. There was an almost audible sigh of relief when the man in the suit invited us into the hall for refreshments.

They could see I was a stranger and they went out of their way to come and talk to me. They were very kind. Frank Russell, I said. He was down at Green Hills. Yes, Russell. No, not Fred, Frank. He was a POW, died on the Burma–Thailand Railway. What they called The Line.

One bloke was nice enough to say, though doubtfully, Oh well, I've heard the name.

Mum would have been heartbroken that Frank left no mark on the world. He hadn't been in the area for long enough and it was too long ago. It was good she wasn't here. There'd have been no sense of *closure*, just a reminder of loss.

I got talking to a nun, standing there with our tilting cups of coffee. How cold it was. Oh, I remember her saying, you want to get a pair of our angora rabbit socks, they'll keep you warm. Rabbit socks, I repeated. I seemed not to be able to make sense of the idea, I felt as if the cold had congealed my brain. I pictured it in my skull, its gleaming grey matter gone viscous and dull like water about to freeze. Yes, the nun said, they shear the rabbits and mix it with the merino.

She glanced around and abruptly said, Well, I'd better go, and just like that she was gone in a flurry of her long skirt. I realised what she'd noticed: we were the only women in the room. Now it was only me. One bloke had cracked open a beer. Someone else had brought out a couple of bottles of Bundy. Would you like a dash? So we're all having a dash of Bundy in our coffee to warm us up.

Then the march. First the soldiers, twenty or thirty men with banners, marching, self-conscious but proud too, medals across their chests. After them a few women walked along, their banner filling in the breeze like a sail, *Something Something Nurses*. Then the fire brigade. The SES. Some other people in uniforms. The Boy Scouts and the Girl Guides, then the Pony Club and the Women's Auxiliary, and by then I'd had enough.

I'm thinking about that freezing morning now. It was a big occasion for this small town, and I think, Good on them for honouring their dead with such sincerity and respect. That man went to a lot of trouble to track down the family of *Russell, F.A.* I should have hung in there till the end of the march, right till the very last stragglers. That would have been the right and courteous thing to do, and I wish I had. But there was a lot of grief that morning. I can see now that the numbness I felt wasn't just the cold. There was grief for poor dead Frank, grief for his life cut short and grief for my mother, who never got over it. When burglars stole Frank's gold fob-watch – *FR* engraved in elaborate letters on the lid – her pain was as raw as the day the telegram had come, regretting that he was dead.

This morning, though, I'm not thinking about Frank. I'm thinking about wars, and how all those memorials in the country towns I've been through on this trip remember the times when men like Frank got on a boat to go and fight far away. The names up in gold are places we might have difficulty finding on a map: *Pozières*, *Tobruk*, *Long Tan*. What I'm thinking now is, what would Australia look like if every country town didn't have only a young man in puttees, but also a memorial for the other war, the one that happened right here at home? If the names up in gold were *Myall Creek, Appin, Forrest River*? After so much damage it might not be possible to list the individual names of the dead, but there'd be some way to make sure the people who'd fought for their homeland were properly remembered.

It's difficult to imagine. Would there be another version of the Dawn Service on a day set aside to honour the dead, everyone coming together to walk down the main street? More reminders up in gold not to forget? And how would it feel to live in a country that could find it in itself to do that?

If there's a place, an actual piece of the earth that's something like sacred ground in our family myths, it's Frank's farm. Green Hills. In my mother's telling of the story, the name of the place was always coloured with sadness, loss, regret.

I'd headed off towards it after the Anzac Day march. It had meant so much to Frank, and to the sister who loved him, and I'd been ready to knock on the door, introduce myself to whoever lived there now. A helpful woman at the newsagent had told me where it was and how to get there, because once again, I hadn't thought to find the exact place on the map. I must have assumed it would be obvious. That uncovering the past wouldn't take work.

The instructions were perfect. There it was, just as she'd said, the red haybarn with a striped painted roof, and opposite it, the gateway without a gate that was Green Hills. I turned in and drove along a track. At the end of it was the house Frank had built – but it was nothing more than a pile of rubble. Knocked down, probably by a bulldozer. It was a dreadful muddle of bricks and dark splintered timbers. I could see pink bathroom tiles and a broken bathroom basin under a jumble of bits of masonite covered with flowery wallpaper. Sheets of twisted roofing-iron. Jagged pieces of mauve glass with a pattern of embossed stars. The wreck of a kitchen cupboard. I could see the smudging around the little black knob where hands had reached to open it. Roses half-smothered in bricks and timber but still showing a few flowers. I touched the soft petals and wondered if Frank had thought about those roses as he laboured under the overseer's whip in Thailand.

The foundations were still there, laid down along the dirt: huge logs, still trees really, round except on the top where they'd been roughly flattened and notched for the joists. I stood for a long time thinking, This is the actual dirt where Frank dragged his boot-heel through the grass to mark a square. He'd have nudged these massive logs into place with a team of horses, hauled and jiggled and checked them with the spirit level until they were near enough, stood back with a mug of tea and looked at the logs lying on the ground, a big square of dirt that would be covered by house and never seen again, until his niece – not even a gleam in anyone's eye when he died – would stand here looking at the ruin.

It was the pink bathroom tiles – those small old-fashioned hexagonal ones – that got to me. I've lived with many a bathroom with tiles like those. I pictured Frank picking them out – there wouldn't have been a lot of choice in Armidale or wherever he'd got them, it would have been blue or pink – putting the glue down on the concrete, lining them up so the sheets of hexagons matched, doing the grout, pleased with the job he'd done. He thought he was building something forever. Building a future. It would be a home, a place to settle and dig in and stay after a childhood spent always moving.

I remember the stab of loss I felt, and how I stood beside that pile of rubble, straining after the actuality of my family on this piece of land. At home I have a tangible memory of that day, an object that I stole. It must have been the emptiness of seeing a precious house reduced to ugly rubble that made me want to take something. The only thing still standing was a shed made of reused roofing-iron. From the jumble of rubbish piled in there I took a long strip of ancient leather with a buckle on one end and a triangular fastening on the other, some bit of harness. The leather's blackened, hard as wood, cracked all over in a pattern like bark. It's a metre long and it's heavy. It hangs in a twist, the leather remembering the shape it took around the flank of a horse. At a pinch, if you knew how, you could still harness up a Clydesdale with it.

There's a photo in the family album of Grandpa in the paddock with his horses. He didn't believe in tractors, he thought they compressed the soil. Frank would have used horses too, would have strapped that bit of harness up morning after morning. Trying to decide whether to take it home with me, I fiddled with the primitive rusty buckle, imagining his hand there, struggling with the harness on a frosty morning, his numb fingers clumsy with the big fastening, cursing in a friendly sort of way, the horse turning its head around to look at the man, steaming breaths of man and horse mingling in the morning air.

I laid the strip of leather along the back seat of the car as if it were a sacred artefact and took it home. It's still there, hanging in the corner of my front porch. There was a feeling of saving something from the wreck. I know taking it was wrong, and I wish I hadn't. That English woman was right – I do have the taint, and not just about a bit of old harness. When I die it will still be there, covered with cobwebs, one more thing for my children to puzzle about.

I'm going to go there again, all these years later, because it's where a certain part of the family story ends. I don't know what I'm expecting, but I suppose I'm hoping for something. I can more or less remember how to get there. Along Ebor Road and then turn right – I'll remember the turnoff when I see it. I seem to remember tennis courts. Yes, there they are, and now I remember the school beside them. And there's something I'd forgotten – a weird high thing that's burst out of the rolling landscape like a huge pimple. The core of an old volcano, I suppose. It's a fair way away but I can see hawks floating above it, watching for the movement in the grass that will mean a mouse for dinner.

If I was ever brought to Green Hills as a child I was too young to remember, but my brother remembers the strange peak over there with the hawks floating over it, remembers the way you had to crack the ice on the washbasin under the tank in the morning to wash your face, and the teatime when he – helpful boy – went to clear the newspapers off the kitchen table and was told to stop. The newspapers were the tablecloth. I've inherited the cupboard with the hole in the back where the rats ate through the wood to get at the food Grandpa kept in it. The whiskey was in there too. After Frank died, Grandpa would have sat by the fire in the kitchen at the newspaper-covered table, staring at the flames with the whiskey in his hand, thinking about his dead son, the wind making that sad sighing in the pines outside.

Even in the car on the way to Green Hills I can feel the wind scouring up from the valley below. I get the feeling it's always like that here, the wind forever blasting up over the slopes. Everywhere there's a house, there's a windbreak of big dark pine trees. Down to the east the ground drops away and there's tufty-looking grass, a few sheep clustered out of the wind in a fold in the hillside.

It's pretty country, but somehow it doesn't speak to me the way other places on this trip have. I don't know what it is that's making me feel out of place and slightly fearful here this time. Maybe it's something about the lumpy grass, and the sombre pines, and the wind.

Frank was living in Queensland when he went in the ballot, and he'd bought the land sight unseen. He'd have driven out on this very road the first day, looking at that strange eruption over there, the hawks drifting over it, and felt the sense of wind and space and cold. At every bend in the road he'd have seen another view of the great windy valley. My guess is he'd have been wondering just what he'd won, and whether it would turn out to be a mistake, like the place just along the road called Ward's Mistake.

Five minutes on it's much as it was twenty years ago, the big red barn and across the road from it the wide gateway, a place on a tongue of high land that pushes out into that valley full of wind. I turn in off the road but this time I don't go any further, because at the end of the track I can see the neat square of a new house.

It's a shock. The pile of broken bricks and twisted roofing-iron was sad, but it was still Frank, still his Green Hills. This place has nothing to do with me. That neat little house shelters people unknown to me, going about their unknown lives. I feel the car rock as the blasts of wind roar over it. I did the wrong thing coming back here. It would have been better to leave the memory intact, sad though it was.

But for heaven's sake, what did I expect? That the place would stay as it was twenty years ago, a shrine to Frank Russell? Or that the wreckage would repair itself and become a loved home once more, with Uncle Frank coming smiling down the steps to greet me?

Last time I was here I spent a long time poking around. The place was gone, but I found it hard to get in the car, turn my back on it, drive away. Today I'm eager to leave. I've got a sense of having come to the end of the road. There are more family stories, of course. About Bert and Dolly in the pubs, about my mother being bullied into becoming a pharmacist, about my own childhood ... but after the story about Green Hills and Frank, the family account of itself shifts gear.

As I drive back up the ridge towards the highway, I feel unsettled, anxious. On edge. Is it the wind, or the lines of spooky dark pines everywhere, or is this what disappointment feels like? It's as if I'm missing some big truth that's staring me in the face, but the more I try to find that big truth the less I can find anything at all. I'm emptied-out, blanked, numbed, a person who has run very hard but still missed what they wanted to catch. I must have been expecting something from Green Hills, some kind of completion or resolution after that long journey through the stories of the four generations and the land. *What do we do, now that we know?* I seem to have come a long way without getting any closer to knowing how to think about that.

But why should I expect anything? What I've done over the last week or so hasn't been a story, with a satisfying narrative arc. I'm not going to go home – as I used to write in my primary school compositions – *tired but happy*, wending my way back down to Sydney with the satisfaction of closure. After all, if you're brutally frank about it, a story is a lovely lie. To make that satisfying narrative arc and that comforting closure, you have to get in there and wrestle reality into shape with your bare hands. You have to be willing to turn your back on some things and make much of others. You have to move things around so they flow nicely, and pick through your vocabulary to find just the right words to generate the emotion you want to generate. You have to ditch digressions and snip off dangling threads. The better the story, the more ruthlessly it's been shaped.

It's wrong to feel disappointed. To expect resolution from this journey is to ask it to be false. A lot has happened. I've seen things in new ways, heard words differently, thought about Aboriginal people in every place I've been. What I've been doing on the trip has really just been one long digression, a whole tapestry of dangling threads, and that's as it should be, because it hasn't been a story, it's been a truth. It's been a provisional, improvised, never-finished journey of feeling, fact, memory, noticing, wondering and learning, and all that is suspended like dust in the air. If it's going to stay true, it has to go on being suspended.

Then, as I go downhill, away from that high windy place with its strange, sad, oppressive mood, I have a sense of coming back to myself. It's suddenly very clear what I'm going to do. The only mystery is why I didn't think of it before. A person who wants to take the first step into knowing *how to be here* might do worse than go to Bingara.

MYALL CREEK

A great deal of the violence that happened on the frontier left nothing more than hints or brief mentions in the written record. But there is an exhaustive account of one massacre, in the form of a court case. The Myall Creek massacre was in its own way uniquely terrible. But in another way, it was representative of what happened, in different circumstances and with different numbers of dead, all over the country.

It took place on a pastoral station called Myall Creek, 150 ks north-west of Tamworth, in 1838. A small group of white men, workers on the place, forced the Aboriginal women, children and old men who were there – about thirty people altogether – into a hut when the younger Aboriginal men were away cutting bark. The men tied up their prisoners, force-marched them a short distance into the bush, and killed them. Then they burned the bodies.

The thing would have faded into the silence of so many similar events of the time, but for the heart of a white man who reported it to a magistrate. The magistrate was a man of heart too, and he investigated. Most unusually, there was a trial. Seven men were eventually convicted and hanged.

It was the first and last time colonists were hanged for the murder of black people. Not because it didn't happen in other times and other places, but because after that the white men were more circumspect – not about what they did, but how they covered it up. After that they probably still made jokes about *accommodating* or *dispersing* Aboriginal people, but they didn't put them down in writing.

The hanging of those seven white men, for the murder of around thirty Aboriginal people, was the start of what's been called the Great Australian Silence about what happened out in the backblocks in the nineteenth and early twentieth centuries. Most balanda Australians can let themselves think that their own forebears weren't involved in any of it. That's if we think about that terrible history at all. It's not so much a matter of *Lest we forget*, more a matter of *Lest we remember.*

Bingara is the town closest to the site of the Myall Creek massacre. Descendants of survivors of the massacre, and descendants of some of the men who did the killing, have lived here since 1838. That could have meant a town divided, a town stiff with silence, a town of pain on one side and self-righteous defensiveness on the other. It hasn't. Instead, in around 2000 those two groups came together – over someone's kitchen table, the story goes – to acknowledge what had happened and make a memorial to it. It wasn't a government initiative, part of some well-meaning Scheme. It was entirely an initiative of the people in a tiny country town, way out in the middle of what many would regard as nowhere. In the beginning, there was no funding or input from any level of government. It was neighbours who knew what had happened far in the past and were prepared to face it.

I've read about the memorial in a casual glance-at-a-piece-in-the-newspaper way. I've got no idea what form it takes. But whatever it is, it's one of the few memorials to the long war that happened right here in Australia. It's certainly the best known. Thousands of visitors every year are prepared to drive a long way to visit it.

As I drive towards the memorial on an afternoon of sunlight and shadow, the windy landscape is alive. Trees bend and gesture like dancers, straining back against themselves, making large gestures with their branches. Fleeting patterns of light and shade ripple across paddocks of long grass. And everywhere, coming towards me down the road, are clusters of tumbleweed striding on long thin legs, end-over-end, a spidery somersaulting that's like an urgent crowd running before the wind.

I turn off the road and come out onto a high, open space, the land falling gently away into a wide valley. There's a sign explaining that the memorial is an *act of reconciliation*.

Reconciliation is an uncomfortably ambiguous word. If you're *reconciled* to something, there's a suggestion that you don't like it, but you've accepted that there's no alternative. You might be *reconciled* to the death of a loved one, but you still wish they were alive. In the context of the frontier wars that's all too appropriate.

First Nations people have been obliged to put up with – reconcile themselves to – what's been imposed on them.

But the other sense of the word is the idea of people coming together after conflict and working through to agreement. There's a happily-ever-after quality to it that doesn't ring true for the wider picture of balanda and First Nations history. There's been plenty of conflict, yes, but not a lot of coming together or working through. *Reconciliation* can feel one-sided, and as if it's been arrived at unearned. When I took part in the Reconciliation Walk over the Sydney Harbour Bridge in 2000, I was very aware of the metaphor: all of us balanda crossing that stretch of deep water without even having to get our feet wet.

Here at Bingara might be one of the few places where the word seems absolutely appropriate. The people in this small community came together and talked things through. That can't have been easy. Together, they devised this memorial. Whatever word you might use for what they did, it's a kind of miracle. For one set of people to look squarely at the wrong their forebears did, for them to own it – and for the other set of people to put aside their rage and hurt and grief – how often, in the history of the world, has such a thing happened? The people here have earned the word.

Nearby, there's another sign:

> The memorial was vandalised in January 2005, with the words "murder", "women" and "children" chiselled off, in an attempt to make it unreadable.

On another day, in another mood, I'd like to think about that. About what's in the mind of someone who brings along a chisel and a hammer, reads the inscription carefully to choose which words are the most powerful, and spends who knows how long, some night, carefully erasing them. I can be pretty sure that that *someone* was a balanda. One of my lot.

It's still possible to live in balanda Australia without knowing how the taking happened. It's taught in schools now, but that's a recent thing. If you're a new arrival, no one tells you about it in the Citizenship Pack. You learn about cricket and mateship. You're not told about massacres or children being torn out of their mothers' arms. And even for people who know, it seems that there are some among us who aren't moved by those facts but provoked to violence by them.

The memorial takes the form of a path. There's a gateway feeling, bushes and rocks shaping themselves to lead you into a winding track. The curves are to remind you that walking along this path isn't about getting from A to B. The curves are to say, You're here for the journey, not the arrival. They say, Slow down, listen, look.

What you hear is the wind in those millions of leaves over your head, the whispering of the long grass, the rustle of the bushes. A bird now and then, and a ticking pulsing from somewhere in the grass. A higher pitch of ticking from the trees. Eternal sorts of sounds, so many tiny living things around you, going about their small lives in this lovely spot.

What you see, at each bend in the track, is a rock with a bronze plaque on it. A big rock, bigger than a person, and as organic. Not shaped, not smoothed, just a tall mass of the fundamental stuff of which the planet is made. One by one the plaques tell the story. It's a horrifying series of events. At any point during that day the white men could have drawn back. One or two did. But, like the path threading its way from plaque to plaque, the events unfolded along their terrible track. It was a long day there by the creek in 1838. Hour by by hour, the white men made their choices. This was no immediate impulse of the moment, rage rising up in a red tide of violence. It was premeditated. The day started with the Aboriginal men going away to cut bark. It ended with a bonfire. That was the only part of the thing that didn't go to plan: the bonfire didn't quite do the job and had to be lit again the next day.

The path ends in a wide clearing, with a rock, bigger than the others, standing in a space of white gravel, surrounded by a circle of stones. There's a final plaque here.

In memory of the Wirrayaraay people who
were murdered on the slopes of this ridge
in an unprovoked but premeditated act in
the late afternoon of 10 June 1838.

Erected on 10 June 2000 by a group of
Aboriginal and non-Aboriginal Australians
in an act of reconciliation, and in
acknowledgment of the truth of our
shared history.

We remember them.

Ngiyani winangay ganunga

The rock stands on the lip of the valley where Myall Creek runs. Beyond, down below somewhere, is the place where the thing actually happened, a piece of the land that holds something for which there can be no words. By now you've journeyed from curve to curve and read the plaques and you know what you need to know. There's no impulse to walk down the slope because you know that down there is sacred land. Down there is set aside, forever marked by what happened. Not a place to be casually walked on. This great guardian rock is as far as anyone should go.

It's a place that invites stillness. A place that strips away the muddle of complications and questions and arguments that are all ways of resisting. Standing in this powerful place, what I'm left with is something very simple. There's a price to pay for being who I am, descended from the people I'm descended from, and part of the price is what I'm allowing myself to feel now. Shame, disgust, horror. Grief, sorrow, a longing for it to have been different.

Over the course of this journey I've come a long way, through geography and through time. I've been on the country that my forebears stole, and in each place I've named it to myself as stolen. The journey's not finished, in fact it's only just started. But I can see this: people like me have to come to belonging not by right, but by a journey into some hard places in the spirit. Learning about what happened in the past is confronting. Shame and sorrow can feel overwhelming. It's an understandable impulse to reject the frightening fact that they're part of our inheritance.

But there's no way forward without acknowledging the things that were done, as the people who devised this memorial have acknowledged them. To know them and to mourn, and to understand that we have to live with what we know. To accept that it's part of who we are. To pick up our grief and sorrow and not look for somewhere to put it down as something that's too heavy for us.

When you learn about the history of the last two hundred years it seems impossible that we can ever go forward from the things that were done. Turning away can seem the only way to deal with them. This memorial is to remember something that feels too dark to look at. But it's also a memorial to what can happen when the dark thing is brought out into the light. Aboriginal and balanda people came together here, looked together at the truth of what took place, and together found a way to go forward. They've shown us that it's not impossible. The rest of us can do it too.

As I start the long drive back home, the power of that site stays with me. I won't forget how it felt to stand there, looking over the valley. But glancing out at the landscape flashing past, I realise that this road trip has shown me another kind of memorial as well. It's quiet, and it's hard to take hold of because it's so big and there's no marked track through it, but it's eloquent. The place itself is a memorial: the ground itself, the actual hills and valleys and rocks and trees and streams of water where the past happened. The truth is right here, right in front of our eyes, still written on the landscape. We just have to look.

ACKNOWLEDGEMENTS

First Nations people are on every page of this book. There are those from the past, among whom are the people dispossessed by my forebears. I honour them and mourn what was done. And there are those from the present, who've been so generous over the years in sharing their knowledge and insights with me, and who've challenged me to look and listen and learn. I thank you.

Historians are also on every page – I couldn't have written it without their careful, honest, often quietly revolutionary work. I was only able to start my thinking because of the place that they make for us: a present that's informed by our knowledge of what's happened in the past.

Many readers engaged with drafts of this book and shared their responses about the places and history I've written about here, and gave wise, thoughtful and knowledgeable advice and comments. I've learned so much from you all, and the book is truer because of your truthful responses. Errors – of judgement and understanding as well as fact – are of course my own.

To put aside one's own work (or play) to engage with another person's book is an act of enormous generosity. I'm immensely grateful to you all.

This book was written on Wurundjeri and Dharawal Country.

These are some of the books that especially guided me as I wrote:

Anna Clark, *Making Australian History*

Callum Clayton-Dixon, *Surviving New England: A History of Aboriginal Resistance and Resilience Through the First Forty Years of the Colonial Apocalypse*

Mark Dunn, *The Convict Valley: The Bloody Struggle on Australia's Early Frontier*

Raimond Gaita, *A Common Humanity: Thinking About Love and Truth and Justice*

Bill Gammage, *The Biggest Estate on Earth: How Aborigines Made Australia*

Stephen Gapps, *The Sydney Wars: Conflict in the Early Colony 1788–1817*

Heather Goodall, *Invasion to Embassy: Land in Aboriginal Politics in New South Wales, 1770–1972*

Ray Kerkhove, *How They Fought: Indigenous Tactics and Weaponry of Australia's Frontier Wars*

Mark McKenna, *Looking for Blackfellas' Point: An Australian History of Place*

David Marr, *Killing for Country: A Family Story*

John Maynard, *Fight for Liberty and Freedom: The Origins of Australian Aboriginal Activism*

Roger Milliss, *Waterloo Creek: The Australia Day Massacre of 1838, George Gipps and the British Conquest of New South Wales*

Bruce Pascoe, *Dark Emu: Aboriginal Australia and the Birth of Agriculture*

Henry Reynolds, *The Law of the Land*

Deborah Bird Rose, *Reports from a Wild Country: Ethics for Decolonisation*

Bernhard Schlink, *Guilt About the Past*

Peter Stanbury and John Clegg, *A Field Guide to Aboriginal Rock Engravings: With Special Reference to Those Around Sydney*

W.E.H. Stanner, *The Boyer Lectures 1968: After the Dreaming*

Jakelin Troy, *King Plates: A History of Aboriginal Gorgets*

Gari Tudor-Smith, Paul Williams and Felicity Meakins, *Bina: First Nations Languages, Old and New*

Judith Wright, *The Cry for the Dead*

A NOTE ABOUT THE TITLE

Many other projects before this book have made use of the rich ambiguities in the word *Unsettled,* among them a 2021 exhibition at the Australian Museum designed by First Nations curators. It's available as a virtual tour on the museum's website, and is an excellent place to start exploring the *unsettling* of the First Nations that balanda *settling* created.